HISTORIC LUCKOW

HISTORIC LUCKNOW

HISTORIC LUCKNOW

SIDNEY HAY

ILLUSTRATED BY
ENVER AHMED

WITH AN INTRODUCTION BY
LORD HAILEY

ISBN : 978-93-5324-585-6 (HB)

First Published, 1939

Published, 2020

Published by

Facsimile Publisher
12 Pragati Market
Ashok Vihar, Ph-2
Delhi-110052
E-mail: books@facsimilepublisher.com

Printed at: G. Print Process, Delhi.

Historic Lucknow

Author: Sidney Hay

HISTORIC LUCKNOW

By SIDNEY HAY

ILLUSTRATED BY
ENVER AHMED

With an Introduction by
THE RIGHT HON. LORD HAILEY, G.C.S.I., G.C.I.E.
Sometime Governor of the United Provinces

LUCKNOW
THE PIONEER PRESS
1939

FOREWORD

I at one time thought that I should like to write a book about Lucknow. It has a personality of its own. It has not, like some of our great cities, a past which runs through the tangled histories of Hindu princedoms and Muslim invasions; it has seen little even of the Great Moguls; but it has in itself all the attractions of a period picture. Its buildings, its records and its traditions are all of the period; its character, as every resident of Oudh knows, was always "Nawabi" and remains "Nawabi". The historian, portraying a dynasty which began with the first great Nawab Wazir and ended with the unhappy Wajid Ali Shah, may see in its record only the story of decline; the artist may find in its buildings much that is artificial and even extravagant. But it is all in character; and its history is so near our own times, and is indeed linked so closely with part of our own record, that it never loses a strong human interest. It is no picture of far-off and half-understood things; we are looking all the time on the Lucknow of the Nawabs with their mixture of Oriental and Western extravagances; the Lucknow of Claud Martin, and above all of Henry Lawrence and the Residency.

When I first read Miss Hay's articles in *The Pioneer* I was glad to find that she was doing something of what I had once hoped to do; and I am delighted to know that we are now to have her articles in book form. It will appeal to all who have known Lucknow and have felt its peculiar charm.

HAILEY.

CONTENTS

CONTENTS—(*concluded*).

HISTORIC LUCKNOW

SA'ADAT KHAN
1732-1739

IN 1705 A PERSIAN LAD NAMED Muhammad Amin set forth with his father and brother from Persia to seek fame and fortune in Hindustan. A Saiyid by birth, he claimed to be a direct descendant of the Prophet himself. He came to Delhi where he attracted the notice of the Emperor of Delhi, Muhammad Shah, then much harassed by the activities of two obstreperous brothers, Abdullah and Hussein Ali, Saiyids of Barhi.

Muhammad Amin, through his ability and business acumen, soon gained power and influence at the court, having been instrumental in assisting the Emperor to overcome the brothers. As a reward, he was given the rank of Burhan-ul-Mulk. In 1720 he became Governor of Agra with the title of Bahadur Jang, when he also assumed the name of Sa'adat Khan.

His executive ability and ambition made him an excellent ruler. In 1732 he was made Governor of Oudh. There he did all in his power to encourage agriculture, at the same time repressing with a stern hand those who threatened to become uncomfortably strong. A forceful and far-sighted ruler, he was also a great warrior. He slew Bhagwant Singh, the Kichi of Fatehpur, in single combat. Even when his long thick beard was white with the passing of years, in battle he was always to be seen wherever the fight was hottest, spurring his men to victory.

He spent much of his time at Delhi in close communication with the Emperor. He built himself a fort at Ajodhya, near Fyzabad, gradually encouraging the state of Oudh to become self-supporting. In time he was able to declare its independence from the Mogul Empire.

Sa'adat Khan decided to visit Lucknow, then called Lakshman Kila, but he met with organised opposition from the Sheikhs, a celebrated and powerful family, several of whom had at one time or another been selected as governors and resented the advent of one with greater authoritative powers. He therefore approached the Akbari Darwaza at the outer city wall. His entry barred, he was obliged to pitch his camp outside the town. He decided on a ruse. He invited all the Sheikhs to a great banquet and when the feasting was at its height he slipped away and entered the city, taking precautions against possible ejection. Over the main gateway the Sheikhs had hung a drawn sword, beneath which they made visitors bow in token of submission. This sword Sa'adat Khan removed. With it went the power of the Sheikhs.

Inside the city were various palaces. Two of these, the Panch Mahal which was five storeys high, and the Mubarak Munzil, or 'Beautiful House,' Sa'adat Khan rented, although it is a moot point whether the owners ever received any payment from him.

He built several more palaces and gardens in Lakshman Kila, a name he altered to Machhi Bhawan "The Fish Fort," to commemorate the Imperial edict which allowed him to assume the now famous fish badge. Beyond the walls of the fort he built Ismailganj, which has since been demolished. Gradually the whole became known as Lucknow, a corruption of Lakshman Kila.

The Nawab-Wazir, as Sa'adat Khan styled himself, was a noble looking man of fine physique, whose flashing eyes brooked no nonsense from his followers. His administrative skill procured him great riches with which to purchase magnificent jewels. He wore upon his head-dress an aigrette mounted upon a superb spray of diamonds. His aquiline nose smelt out any treachery which threatened him. His skin, rippling over the sturdy muscles, was fair. He had tact, ability and courage, but he was cruel and treacherous.

In 1739 he betrayed his benefactor, the Mogul Emperor, to Nadir Shah, joining forces with the latter in Delhi, where he became Wazir of the Delhi Empire the same year. He did not live long to enjoy the fruits of his treachery, for he was poisoned a few months later, either by his enemies, or by his own hand in a fit of remorse. He died in Delhi, where he was buried.

His ally, Nadir Shah, bled him of many large sums of money. In spite of this Sa'adat Khan left his successor a well-filled treasury containing nearly fifteen crores of rupees.

SAFDAR JANG
1739—1753

FAMOUS THROUGHOUT INDIA AS SAFDAR Jang, the real name of the second Nawab of Oudh was Abul Mansur Khan, or Ali Mansur Khan. He was the nephew and son-in-law of Sa'adat Ali Khan, his predecessor. The name of his wife was Begum Aliya Sadru.

The Emperor of Delhi, Muhammad Shah, was engaged in a war in Sirhind against Shah Abdali when his commander, Mirza Ahmad, was joined by Safdar Jang and a number of guns ; with his aid Shah Abdali was defeated three times.

On the death of the Emperor in 1749 Mirza Ahmad succeeded to the throne of Delhi, whereupon Safdar Jang, then Subadar of Oudh, followed the example of his uncle, displaying his talents at the court to such advantage that he was soon made Wazir of the Delhi Empire, an office which thenceforth became hereditary. It was usual for a Subadar to rule his 'suba' in the country, while his duties of Wazir were performed in Delhi by a deputy.

Safdar Jang, being of a militant disposition, warred against the Rohillas. By enlisting Maratha aid he temporarily subdued the Pathans before he took up his abode in Oudh and established his court at Fyzabad.

He continued to rent the palaces taken by his predecessor in Lucknow and finally assumed complete possession by exchanging them with a Sheikh family for seven hundred acres of land in Dugaon. He did not reside permanently in Lucknow, however, until almost towards the end of his life, but his financial ability strengthened his already influential position as ruler of Oudh. As a visible sign of his wealth and power, he built the fort of Jalalabad in the direction of Cawnpore, not far from Lucknow. This fort has lately fallen into complete ruin. It was the scene of sharp fighting in 1858, for it came into the line of defences which also included the Alam Bagh.

On January 12, 1858, the rebels planned a great attack upon General Outram's force, and a Hindu fanatic who purported to represent Hanuman, the monkey god, led a large body of men against Jalalabad. They were repulsed and left their leader and many of their comrades dead upon the field. Another massed attack was made upon the same line of defences on February 21. This also failed. Soon Jalalabad Fort was abandoned as lacking in strategical importance, for the field of activity of the British narrowed as they succeeded in quelling disturbances.

To return to the reign of Safdar Jang, his minister Newal Rai planned the great stone bridge over the Gumti at Lucknow, but died before it could be completed.

Authorities differ as to dates about this time, but it is generally accepted that Safdar Jang died of fever in 1753. His remains were taken to Delhi, where they were interred beneath the world-famous edifice known as Safdar Jang's Tomb, to this day a place of beauty, whether sparkling in the glory of the mid-day sun, silhouetted against the soft grey half-light of evening, or silent in the mysterious radiance of the moon.

In appearance Safdar Jang was a fine-looking man. Like his uncle he wore a beard and possessed clear-cut features and an aristocratically high-bridged nose. His garments were of the finest material. Although he did not display a great number of jewels, those he wore were large and valuable. In his best-known portrait he is shown as wearing a long white robe with a swinging skirt, not unlike that of a dancing girl. Girded at the waist was a belt which held his sword in a velvet scabbard, richly ornamented. His corsage was relieved by ropes of precious stones. Over all he wore a richly embossed coat, heavy bracelets jangling at either wrist. The *pagri* was loosely tied, a long aigrette fastened at the front and curled over his head. This portrait, which was executed some years after his death, contains an anachronism, for in the background is the great Chutter Munzil Palace which was not built until more than half a century later !

SHUJA-UD-DOULAH
1753—1775

SAFDAR JANG WAS SUCCEEDED on the throne by his son Shuja-ud-Doulah, famed far and wide for his good looks and military talents which were augmented by Herculean strength. Yet from a full length portrait, judged by modern standards, he would not be deemed an Adonis. His face was long, with fat cheeks terminating in deep lines from nostril to mouth. A pair of moustaches, which on each side measured some four inches in length, added to his mien an air of ferocity already imparted by a pair of sharp, close-set eyes. Fashions had changed from his father's day. Although he still wore a full skirt, it was shortened to the calf, showing a pair of top boots. The cut-away coat was trimmed with fur. He wore many fine jewels. His head-dress appears to have been made of fur, secured with a circlet of precious stones. He carried a long thin sword.

About 1760, Shuja-ud-Doulah was made Wazir of the Delhi Empire by the Emperor Shah Alam, thus carrying on the family tradition. He joined forces with the Emperor to march against the British in the name of Mir Kasim, who had been displaced from the office of Governor of Bengal. In November 1763, Mir Kasim had fled to Oudh, where Shuja-ud-Doulah accorded him a warm welcome. At the battle of Buxar on October 25, 1764, however, they were heavily defeated by the Company's troops under the command of Major Hector Munro. This battle finally established the supremacy of the East India Company to whom Shuja-ud-Doulah had to surrender. The Company did not then wish to extend its sphere of jurisdiction, and so in 1765 a treaty was concluded at Allahabad by which the Nawab was reinstated in his province with the exception of the districts of Allahabad and Korah. The Company declared that it would assist him with such forces as the exigencies of his affairs might require, but that should such occasion arise, all attendant expenses would be borne by the Nawab-Wazir. This treaty was the result of a personal interview between Lord Clive and Shuja-ud-Doulah. Gradually the state grew more and more dependent upon the military assistance of the East India Company. As the French menace grew increasingly acute, Oudh clung the closer to her strong English ally; although in 1775 Warren Hastings wrote that under certain conditions nothing could prevent the Marathas laying waste the province of Oudh, in spite of attempts of the European soldiery to stop them.

Opinions have been expressed that the East India Company treated Oudh badly by ignoring various treaty clauses, but the fact is that it was doing its best to combat the French, and actually it supported Shuja-ud-Doulah loyally.

In 1768 the Nawab agreed to keep an army of a strength not exceeding 35,000 men. Five years later Mr. Nathaniel Middleton was appointed as the first British Resident in Oudh, thus virtually asserting British supremacy. At the same time a brigade, consisting of two European and six sepoy battalions and a company of Artillery, was sent to Oudh and maintained at the Nawab's expense. The troops were stationed at Faizpur Kampu, between two and three miles from Belgram. In 1781, long after the barracks had disappeared, the names persisted in the fields, which were still called the *Kamsariat* (provisions), *Kabarahar* (cemetery) and *Gendkhana* (cricket ground).

Shuja-ud-Doulah lived in Fyzabad where he died in 1775 at the early age of forty-six. There he was buried beneath an imposing mausoleum. Latterly he had lived in Lucknow, as being more central, but it was left to his successors finally to transfer the capital city there from Fyzabad.

Jis ko na de Maula
Usko de Asaf-ud-Doulah
(To whom God does not give
To him Asaf-ud-Doulah gives.)

ASAF-UD-DOULAH
1775—1798

ASAF-UD-DOULAH IS REMEMBERED to this day in Lucknow for his unlimited generosity.

When Shuja-ud-Doulah died in 1775, his son Mirza Amani became Nawab, assuming the name of Asaf-ud-Doulah. In the same year, he transferred his capital from Fyzabad to Lucknow and at once set on foot schemes for the aggrandisement of his new headquarters, for Lucknow was then not much more than a large village. He and his courtiers lived in the Daulat Khana behind the Taluqdars' Hall in the Husainabad area while his other schemes were taking shape.

To him are attributed the Rumi Darwaza, the Great Imambara and the Bibiapur Kothi. The magnificence and wealth of his court enhanced his fame until it exceeded that of the Great Mogul himself, living not so far away at Delhi. Adventurers, hearing of the riches and luxury to be had almost for the asking, crowded to the' court of Lucknow.

During this reign the fame and luxury of Oudh reached its zenith. No other kingdom throughout the length and breadth of India could rival it. The Nawab's only apparent ambition was to discover how many elephants the Nizam or Tippu Sultan possessed, how valuable were their diamonds—and then to surpass them. His vast wealth was collected from the peasants who were fleeced by officials until they were put almost out of existence.

Six months after his accession Asaf-ud-Doulah ceded Jaunpur and Ghazipur to the British with an annual payment to the Company. He then applied for, and received, the services of several Europeans to officer his troops. Shortly after they had assumed command of the army a mutiny broke out and a fierce engagement was fought between 2,500 matchlockmen and 15,000 regulars. This only ended when a tumbril exploded and the rebel forces retreated, leaving 600 mutineers and 300 regulars dead on the battle-field.

Asaf-ud-Doulah heard of an enterprising young Frenchman named Claud Martin, whose inventive mind had, amongst other things, caused the first balloon in India to ascend into the air. This intrigued the Nawab who asked that Martin might be transferred to his service. The request was granted. From that time began Martin's days of wealth, prosperity, and power. When he came to Lucknow he took over the Hayat Baksh Kothi, the present Government House, as an arsenal. There he established "a manufactory where he makes pistols and fusils both as to lock and barrel better than the best arms that come from Europe." He was clever and a faithful servant to the Nawab, and effected many excellent reforms in the military machinery of the state.

Portraits show Asaf-ud-Doulah as a squarely built man of portly mien, with protruding eyes and pendulous moustaches. His dress, of the finest white muslin, reached to his instep and was very full, bordered by rich metal braid. Long sleeves were caught at wrist and upper arm by bands of embroidery. His closely wound turban was overlaid with plaques of precious stones, surmounted by valuable aigrettes. About his waist wound a thick scarlet-and-gold cord into which was thrust a large jewelled dagger.

When the fame of the Court of Oudh was firmly established, an English artist named William Hodges, who had been a member of Captain Cook's expedition to the South Seas, visited India, where he secured the patronage of Warren Hastings. In company with another artist, John Zoffany, who was then coming to the end of his monetary resources in England, and who had obviously been stirred by the extravagant tales of wealth at the court of Oudh, Hodges set sail in 1783. The two artists landed at Calcutta, whence they made their way up-country to Lucknow. Hodges did not make much headway but Zoffany quickly established a reputation for himself, and in 1784 he painted a portrait of the Nawab, inscribed: "John Zoffany painted this picture at Lucknow A.D. 1784 by order of His Highness the Nawab Vizier Asoph-ud-doulah, who gave it to his servant Francis Baladon Thomas."

Zoffany immortalised a favourite sport of the day in what is, perhaps, his best-known picture, 'Colonel Mordaunt's Cock Match', painted in 1786. In this picture appears a portrait of the Nawab and of other well-known contemporaries, both Indian and European.

During Asaf-ud-Doulah's reign seven British Residents successively assisted in the administration of his lands and revenue. In 1794 one Thomas Twining of the Civil Service accompanied the Commander-in-Chief of the Company's army on a tour of inspection.

On January 5, 1795, Twining wrote: "I dined to-day with Mr. Orr, an English merchant, and met a large party of English gentlemen, among whom was Dr. James Laird, brother of the head physician who accompanied Sir Robert Abercrombie from Calcutta. There were also Mr. Paul and Mr. and Mrs. Arnot. Mrs. Arnot enjoys the distinction of being the handsomest lady in India."

Mr. Orr was a rich merchant who resided for many years in Lucknow, besides possessing a bungalow at Tanda near Fyzabad, where also were situated one of his several cotton cloth factories. Twining was agreeably impressed with Lucknow society for he wrote that "the style in which this remote colony lived was surprising, it far exceeding even the expense and luxuriousness of Calcutta.

As it was the custom of these families to dine alternately with each other they had established a numerous band of musicians."

Of the Nawab himself, Twining noted that "in polished and agreeable manners, in public magnificence, in private generosity, and also, it must be allowed, in wasteful profusion, Asaf-ud-Doulah, Nawab of Oudh, might probably be compared with the most splendid sovereign of Europe."

The Nawab had a great admiration for things European and things mechanical. In a building known as the Ina Khana he made a collection of objects which, so long as they were English, needed no other common denominator. Watches, clocks, scientific instruments, fire-arms, glass, and furniture were jumbled together in utter confusion. Timepieces studded with jewels and exquisitely ornamented in coloured enamels lay cheek by jowl with the most tawdry imitations. Each had probably cost the Nawab an equal sum of money, and each had presumably caught his attention for a similar number of minutes. Above this quaint muddle of trumpery and jewels hung a myriad crystal prisms, reflecting the light diffused from a number of wall and table lamps set here and there with little thought of artistry.

In 1784 a famine came upon Lucknow. As a relief measure and to give employment to his people, Asaf-ud-Doulah caused architects throughout India to submit plans for a building to be known as the Great Imambara.

But the Nawab, although he built great palaces, laid out beautiful gardens and sank wells, had no eye for the squalor of his immediate surroundings. The city itself was a miserable place; the streets were narrow, dirty, and crowded with bazaars and very poor people. "It was evident," writes one spectator, "that splendour was confined to the palace while misery pervaded the streets: the true image of despotism."

In spite of this the Nawab was held in affection by his subjects until the day of his death and was laid to rest beneath the high vaulted ceiling of the Great Imambara, for which, rumour has it, over a million English pounds bought the ornate chandeliers and mirrors to complete the state's bankruptcy.

As a result of extravagance and lack of supervision over petty court officials and tax-collectors, the court of Oudh found itself almost penniless at the death of Asaf-ud-Doulah in 1798.

WAZIR ALI—INTERLOPER
1798

When Asaf-ud-Doulah, fourth Nawab of Oudh, died in 1798, his continued extravagances were found to have left finances in a precarious condition. Two years before his death, Haider Beg Khan, his Prime Minister, had died. The Nawab, who cared nothing for administration or the welfare of his people, then allowed the state to lie at the mercy of any money-grabber who chanced along. Finally, in 1797 Sir John Shore visited Lucknow and persuaded the Nawab to appoint Tafazzul Hussain as his minister, a trustworthy and astute man who could be relied upon to do his best to pull things together. A few months later Asaf-ud-Doulah died, leaving no legitimate heir. Many years before, however, he had bought a child named Wazir Ali whom he had brought up as his own son, but whom he had never taken the trouble legally to adopt. However, nobody seemed to regard this as a deterrent to his ascending the throne of Oudh. Not only did he do so, but he also obtained the consent of the Resident, Mr. John Lumsden, and of the Governor-General, Sir John Shore.

Wazir Ali turned out to be a man whose vices rivalled those of his adopted father. He had an uncontrollable temper which was easily aroused and greatly disliked English interference.

During the coronation year, Tennant visited Lucknow, of which he remarked that the outskirts of the city and the areas far removed from the royal palaces were indescribably filthy and wretched. For nearly three miles the main street was a sea of mud and filth, and really amounted to little more than a sewer, the centre twelve feet lower than the edges and too narrow to permit of more than one line of wheeled traffic. Vice, debauchery and poverty stalked the streets to the exclusion of prosperity; for only those who had the fortune to be attached to the court had any pretensions to wealth.

The Minister, Tafazzul Hussain, reported to the British, who had installed him in his post, that the scenes of debauchery were growing even more frequent since the accession of Wazir Ali.

The result was that Sir John Shore himself again visited Lucknow to institute a thorough and careful inquiry into the reigning Nawab's antecedents. It was conclusively proved that he had no shadow of claim to the throne of Oudh and so four months after his accession he was deposed and sent to Benares. Wazir Ali is omitted from chronicles referring to the rulers of Oudh, and consequently his portrait does not hang with those of every Nawab and King of Oudh in the Taluqdars' Hall in the Husainabad Park.

In his stead the Governor-General sent for Sa'adat Ali, a half-brother of Asaf-ud-Doulah, who had been living under British protection at Benares since 1776.

SA'ADAT ALI KHAN
1798—1814.

OUDH WAS IN A BAD WAY. Money had run through Asaf-ud-Doulah's fingers like water. After his death matters continued in the same way during the four months when Wazir Ali sat feebly upon the throne, with no thought for anything but debauchery. Then came Sa'adat Ali Khan, half-brother of Asaf-ud-Doulah.

But matters did not improve. Sa'adat Ali had possibly inherited that same strain of extravagance which had earlier been shown by his brother. Or, perhaps, sudden access to luxury, a title, and the semblance of wealth, however unsubstantial, went to his head. At any rate, life at the court of Lucknow continued as before. Ever more pressing and more insistent became the bills and notes of promise. So loud were the voices shouting for payment that they eventually reached the ears of the King himself. Troubles gathered thick and fast about Sa'adat Ali, until he knew not what to do. His troops were useless. There were continual and mutinous mutterings from the sepoys displeased at the abrupt departure of Wazir Ali who had included the army in his distribution of money not his to give.

Sultan Tippu of Mysore and his ally Zaman Shah were turning their thoughts and their armies towards the boundaries of Oudh. Sa'adat Ali looked in his distress to the strongest person he could think of—the Governor-General, Lord Wellesley. The latter declared that the Nawab's army must be disbanded and replaced by the Company's troops. The Nawab in his terror gladly agreed, but, as his fears abated, tried to back out of the agreement. Lord Wellesley stood firm, however, and the place of the unruly rabble was filled by twelve battalions of infantry and four regiments of cavalry, costing fifty lakhs a year to maintain.

This increased the annual payment due to the Company to 126 lakhs a year. The Governor-General proposed a scheme whereby the exclusive civil and military government of the state should be transferred to the Company. The Nawab flatly refused to consider this. Rather than be a figurehead, a useless puppet, he would abdicate. The alternative was to cede to the Company territory to yield a substantial part of his revenue.

Finally, in 1801, after much discussion, an agreement was reached whereby Sa'adat Ali Khan should hand to the Company certain of his lands which became known as the Ceded Provinces, and which formed the beginnings of the present province of Agra. In addition, the fort of Allahabad was to be used as an arsenal by the Company's troops.

The solemnity of the proceedings went deep into Sa'adat Ali's heart, for he made a pilgrimage to the sacred Dargah of Hazrat Abbas in Lucknow. There he made a solemn vow before the shrine to abstain from all indulgence and debauchery of the flesh, and to give his whole attention to the right governing of his country. This vow he kept, and no sovereign of Oudh has conducted the Government with as great ability as he did for the remaining fourteen years of his life.

His portraits show him to be portly, tall and with several chins. He was clean shaven save for a small ferocious moustache. His nose was straight and aquiline and large ears protruded on either side of a wide head illuminated by suspicious-looking hazel eyes. His head-dress was formed of rolls of costly material tightly wound into a sort of hat. He wore a long brocade robe, beneath which soft and full silken trousers fell over his gold shoes with their curved points. About his waist was twisted a broad sash. He carried a long curved scimitar sheathed in purple velvet, the hilt studded with precious stones. Round his neck he wore two or three rows of enormous jewels.

Sa'adat Ali Khan had spent his youth in Calcutta surrounded by

Europeans. He had assimilated many of their ideas and methods. Some say that he spoke English perfectly ; others that he could understand, read and write, but not pronounce. In any case, his devotion to, and admiration for, the Company were strong and continued throughout his life. He set about introducing reforms with a right good will. He reorganised the collection of revenue. He made large grants of land to worthy aspirants. He took pains to protect the agriculturists.

In spite of his economies, he lived in a manner befitting a King. In 1805 a lady described his usual way of living. He kept a table which, both in appointments and in the fare provided, could vie with any belonging to men of rank in England. There were three separate dishes provided for each course. That at the upper end of the table was cooked by an English cook; that in the centre by an Indian; and that at the lower end was prepared by a French chef. The Nawab owned a set of Worcestershire china, complete in every detail, for dining-room, bedroom and bath-room. He and his retainers did not gauge the function of every unit of the sets, with the result that a certain article of bedroom furniture was placed upon the dinner-table filled with milk. The Nawab, knowing that his English guests liked that beverage, could not fathom why they touched none.

Except when he gave splendid and lavish banquets, Sa'adat Ali lived sparingly. His personal habits were frugal and economical, so that he earned a somewhat unjust reputation for parsimony and miserliness. But he gained an entirely new character during the latter and greater part of his reign as being the best administrator and the most sagacious ruler that Oudh had ever seen : a character which stood out the more sharply against a background of the lavish extravagances of his brother, the former Nawab.

Gradually he developed Lucknow towards the east and although "the city of Lucknow, excepting the Nawab's palaces, is neither so large nor so splendid as that of Benares," it was he who built the cantonment of Mariaon across the river, his favourite shooting box of Dilkusha, the imposing structures of the Moti Mahal, the great Chaupar stables (Lawrence Terrace), and many other structures which are still preserved to-day.

He himself lived in the Farhat Bakhsh which he purchased from General Claud Martin. As early as 1801 he established a reserve treasury which grew to fourteen crores of rupees at his death.

In 1814, the last year of his reign, Lord Hastings honoured him with a visit. The royal apartments were unpretentious, yet they conveyed an air of comfort. Breakfast, in those days a meal to which guests were often invited, was held in a spacious house built in the Saracenic style and protected from the fierce sun by commodious awnings. The meal consisted of tea or coffee, pilau, Indian dishes and ices. Dancing girls entertained the guests during the meal. The King's father had insisted that Sa'adat Ali Khan should never touch intoxicants. From the quality of the liquor kept, it seemed fairly certain that the father's wish was respected.

For all his sensible ways, the Nawab had one or two idiosyncrasies. For instance, he refused to repair the noble old stone bridge spanning the Gumti, saying that should he mend it in any way it would cause his death within the year. Similarly, in 1810 he ordered from England an iron bridge, the first of its kind to reach India, but for some reason he refused to erect it and it lay by the side of the river, still in the packing cases in which its sections had travelled from England, for nearly forty years.

Presumably Sa'adat Ali preferred to keep the reins of government within his own grasp, for his little son who had certainly not reached years of discretion was proclaimed Chief Justice. In this capacity he had to escort honoured guests to the Royal banquets. On one occasion the lady whom he came to squire kept him waiting. It was late in the evening, after a hot and tiring day, and the poor child fell asleep in the ante-room. Promptly his attendant gentleman woke him up, took him aside, and whipped him soundly for committing so gross a breach of ceremonial observance.

On July 11, 1814, Sa'adat Ali Khan died by poisoning, aged about sixty. His remains lie in the larger of the two domed mausoleums near Aminabad. Beside him, beneath the lesser edifice, lies his chief wife, Kurshaed Zadi.

Actually when he died the site where he now lies was occupied by his son's palace, but the son, Ghazi-ud-Din Haider, who succeeded him, declared that it was only meet that, as he had taken his father's place, his father should have his. Whereupon he pulled down his palace to build his father's tomb upon the spot.

Sa'adat Ali left behind him nine sons. One died in the same year as his father, but an Oudh paper dated 1837 shows that at that time five of them were still alive in spite of the cruelties of their great-nephew, the notorious Nasir-ud-Din Haider, to whom nothing gave more delight than to torment the aged, the infirm, and the helpless.

GHAZI-UD-DIN HAIDER
1814—1827

Although Nawab Sa'adat Ali Khan himself had been "westernised" and understood English, he took no interest in the education of his sons, who grew up ill-equipped to take their place as leaders of society. Indeed, his second son, Ghazi-ud-Din Haider, who succeeded him upon the throne, spoke no English and was entirely unversed in court usage. He was, however, fond of study, and in oriental philology and philosophy he was reckoned learned. He had a strong taste for mechanics and chemistry and employed an Englishman named Thomas Denham as chief mechanic and Mr. Tucket as architect and engineer.

His court became remarkable both for splendour and for agreeable and polished manners. He showed a lively interest in literature and the arts and did much to encourage and support those around him who showed talent. He appointed Mr. Robert Home, a well-known English artist, to be his historical and court painter. The artist stayed at Lucknow for many years, ultimately dying in Cawnpore.

For some months after Ghazi-ud-Din's accession, Hakim Mehdi, Sa'adat Ali Khan's trusted minister, remained in office. But by dint of continuous intrigue, an unscrupulous but able man named Agha Mir supplanted him and gained complete political mastery over the Nawab. He "took from the country the annual sum of twenty-three million rupees by his own admission, and three million three hundred thousand agreeably to the accounts in the office. The property and jewels of the state which he plundered are out of the question," and all this in addition to his monthly salary of Rs. 25,000. He refused to carry out any reforms suggested by the British, with the result that abuses of authority again crept in, and the country gradually sank back into the poverty from which his predecessor had so laboriously raised it. So complete was his mastery over the Nawab that he prevailed upon him to imprison for a time Nasir-ud-Din Haider, the heir presumptive, on a trumpery charge.

Ghazi-ud-Din Haider was not an inspired builder like his father, but he constructed the Chutter Munzil Palaces, the Mubarak and Shah Munzils, the Qadam Rasul, the Walaiti Bagh, and was responsible for the now extinct irrigation canal system, besides the Shah Najaf, his own tomb. During his reign he lived in the Farhat Bakhsh, which was built by General Claud Martin at the end of the previous century. There he died.

His chief wife, Badshah Begum, was possessed of a violent temper. After his death she became a well-known character who in stilled submission into all and sundry by virtue of her rough and ready tongue—no mean achievement for a woman in those days of purdah. Early in 1818 Lord Hastings, the Governor-General, visited Lucknow for the second time. He records that he treated the Nawab-Wazir with the respect accorded to a reigning sovereign of high rank. Ghazi-ud-Din Haider gave a state banquet in honour of the Governor-General, followed by a durbar.

The Nawab desired to present to the Governor-General a crore of rupees for the use of the Government, but this the latter would not allow, and would only take it on loan upon a small rate of interest. Not long afterwards Ghazi-ud-Din again produced money to meet the expenses of the war with Nepal. In 1819 the Marquess of Hastings once more visited Lucknow and conferred upon the Nawab the title of King.

A portrait of Ghazi-ud-Din hung at one time in the Dilkusha palace. A portrait now hanging in the Taluqdars' Hall depicts him dressed in his robes of state, resting upon a sword, and surrounded by his courtiers, as a fine-looking man with well marked features and elegant, artistic hands. Upon his head is a large jewelled crown. About his neck is clasped a wide collar studded with priceless jewels. Over his rich robe of brocade he wears a flowing velvet court cloak lined with ermine, with an ermine collar clasped about his throat by a jewelled fastening. Over this again hangs a wonderful chain similar to a modern mayoral chain, but far more magnificent and costly.

Bishop Heber described him in 1824 as being tall, his body long in proportion to his legs, and with distinct evidence of having been extremely good-looking. He had aged earlier than most men of his years and his greying hair sat strangely above an unusually dark skin. He was spruce and well turned out and liked to see his courtiers likewise. His tastes had been well directed in his youth and he had collected in his palaces many beautiful things, both oriental and European. He was wont to treat European ladies, to their chagrin, exactly as he would his own women—as being of no account whatever. He soon saw through the endless variety of importunate adventurers of every class, colour and creed who found their way to his court in the hope of obtaining employment. In spite of this he had many Europeans and half-castes in his employ.

Bishop Heber was once invited to breakfast with the King. Writing to his wife, he described in detail his excursion into the royal presence. The Bishop, in company with the British Resident, arrived at the palace in a palanquin. There they were deposited at the foot of an unimposing staircase built in stone. At the head of this stood the King, waiting to receive his guests, which he did by kissing them resoundingly. He conducted them into a picture gallery equipped with fine crystal chandeliers and furnished in European style. In the centre of the room a large oblong dining-table was set with Western china, at which the party seated themselves in strict order of precedence. There they sat until the King set the proceedings in motion by grabbing two large hot rolls which he presented, one to the Bishop and one to the Resident. This was the signal for the servants to hand coffee, tea, butter, eggs and fish to the guests, all of whom, including the Muhammadans, ate in European fashion, and of European fare, except the royal host himself who consumed some special dish of his own served in a bowl of exquisite French design.

The King died in 1827 at his Lucknow palace, leaving his treasury well lined with a reserve of four crores of rupees. He lies buried in the Shah Najaf where may still be seen a number of interesting relics of his reign.

NASIR-UD-DIN HAIDER
1827—1837

FOLLOWING TRADITION, the second King of Oudh, who succeeded to the throne in 1827, changed his name from Suleman Jah to Nasir-ud-din Haider.

King Ghazi-ud-Din Haider died—and it is significant of the violent deeds prevalent in those days that historians add that he died "a natural death"—on October 20, 1827, to be succeeded by one whom he had declared to be his son by a slave girl, but who was popularly reputed to be the son of a washerman attached to the palace. This rumour is supported by a document which states that "Ghazee-ood-Deen had no son and only one daughter, who married her cousin and had issue Mossem-ood-Doulah, the true heir to the throne. Ghazee-ood-Deen, instead of leaving the throne to his true heir and grandson Mossem-ood-Doulah, left it to Nuseer-ood-Deen Hydeer." Moreover, Colonel Low, the British Resident in Lucknow, wrote a memorandum saying that a letter was intercepted from the Padshah Begum addressed to the late Mr. Secretary Stirling to the effect that Nasir-ud-Din Haider was not the rightful heir, nor even the son of Ghazi-ud-Din Haider.

Although Nasir appeared to inherit none of the dignity and kingly qualities of his predecessor, a love of mechanics characterised them both. He built and equipped the Tara Wala Kothi, or observatory, which he placed under the charge of Colonel Wilcox. He was much interested in steamers, then a recent invention even in Europe. So interested was he that he bought and placed upon the Ganges one of these new-fangled contraptions in order to make occasional excursions. The Bengal Steam Navigation Fund enjoyed his liberal support in return for keeping him informed of current developments. He employed a succession of European artists of note as his court painters, among them Robert Home and George Beechey. The latter was also made Comptroller of the King's Household. Indeed, Nasir-ud-Din surrounded himself with Europeans wherever possible and was at the mercy of any degenerate rascal who happened to come along so long as he was a European. Chief among these was the notorious barber, de Russet, who was said to have fleeced the King of no less than 24 lakhs of rupees.

Nasir-ud-Din who had no proper conception of his kingly responsibilities cared only for amusements, and his tastes grew more and more degenerate with the passing of time.

He took as his chief wife Sultana Boa, the grand-daughter of the Emperor Shah Alam. But when she realised what manner of man he was, she cut herself off from him and lived in seclusion. Another of his wives was a Miss Walters, daughter of George Hopkins Walters, a retired servant of the Company. She held his attention for some years during which she wheedled considerable wealth from him. She married him in 1827 and died in November 1830. The house in which her mother, then Mrs. Wheatley, and elder sister lived stands to this day within the Residency enclosure where it is known as the Begum Kothi. The elder unmarried daughter was known as the Begum Ashraf-un-Nisa, whilst the younger one who married the King became a Muhammadan and took the name of Jukuddera Queela.

Still another woman was raised from the status of an infant's nurse to that of chief consort. She became known as Malika Jamani, or Queen of the Age, when she married the King. Her son, Kywan Jah, already three years old before she entered the palace by the front door, the King insisted upon nominating as his heir.

The King had originally peculiarly lank straight hair, and not an approach to a curl had ever been seen therein. The barber, de Russet, wrought wonders during a chance visit from Calcutta and the King was delighted. Honours and wealth were showered upon the lucky coiffeur. So much did Nasir-ud-Din come to lean upon him that he trusted de Russet to see that every bottle of wine was sealed in the barber's house before being brought to the royal table. Before he opened it, the little man carefully inspected the seal to see that all was well. He then opened it, took a sip himself, and poured out a glass for the King.

In the Lucknow museum stands a bronze bust of King Nasir-ud-Din Haider, showing a sensual, almost feminine, countenance with full lips, the whole framed in luxuriant curls, upon which rests a fine massive crown. It is interesting to compare this bust with an earlier portrait showing him with a firmer mouth, his hair short and severely straight, as it was before the ministrations of de Russet. He wears in both pictures the same ermine robe of state, the same jewelled collar, and the same wondrous chain of gems, and what must be the same crown, although in one or the other it has been carelessly copied, for the details are dissimilar.

Animal fights were a fashionable court pastime of the day, especially when the combatants were elephants or quails. The fights of the former took place near the Moti Mahal palace, and those of the latter upon the King's dinner table after a banquet.

King Nasir-ud-Din Haider had that shrewd cunning often associated with the possessor of a weak intellect. He was quick to see slights whether or not they were intended. On the other hand, he was easily delighted with childish games if he was assured they were popular among European children. Leap-frog took his fancy and, although he collapsed when trying to "make a back" or when he failed to clear a back bent for him, it was not through lack of effort. He had heard from the Englishmen surrounding him about the fox's brush as a trophy at the end of a run. Not to be outdone, he set his cheetahs coursing after deer. At the end of the chase, having followed on horseback, he secured the tail of a deer, attached it to the front of his cap, and rode home in triumph.

Year by year the power of the barber steadily grew. He could do no wrong in the King's eyes. Nobody dared gainsay him. But year by year the King grew more capricious and, at last, after a more than usually strong representation from the British Resident, Nasir-ud-Din exclaimed in a fit of rage to de Russet that he had driven away the only good counsellors in the state. The barber saw that his reign of influence was about to end, wisely gathered together all the valuables he could muster and fled from the kingdom into the Company's territory.

After his departure the King was more rudderless than ever. His fear of poisoning grew overwhelming. All his drinking water he drew from a small well in the palace, kept free from contamination by being under his own lock and key. He always locked away the jar in which he drew his own water. The persons who ministered to his thirst, save when the water came from English sealed bottles, were two sisters, Dhuneea and Dulwee.

Gradually aliens were introduced into the ranks of the palace servants. Four months after the barber's departure, the King died by drinking poisoned sharbat—the very thing of which he had been most afraid—on July 8, 1837. He was interred in the *kerbala* built by himself at Iradat Nagar on the north bank of the Gumti.

MUHAMMAD ALI SHAH
1837—1842

When King Nasir-ud-Din Haider died by an unknown hand, drinking poisoned sharbat as he lay on his bed of silken cushions in the Farhat Bakhsh palace, the country had passed into such a state that anything might happen. Five years before, the British Government had instructed Colonel Low, the Resident, to uphold Nasir-ud-Doulah, one of the

King's uncles, as his successor. Directly the news of the King's death was brought, Colonel Low hurried down the slope which led from the Residency to the palace. Nasir-ud-Doulah was informed and escorted with all possible speed to the palace where he arrived at about three in the morning of July 8, only a few hours after Nasir-ud-Din had passed away. He was even then an old man and infirm, and this rude awakening in the middle of the night did not suit him; so he retired unnoticed to a small room in the palace until morning.

Meanwhile the Resident took a firm grip of affairs at the palace, for he was expecting trouble. He placed his escort as sentries at every entrance of the palace, and a corps of Oudh Infantry took post at the main southern gate. Preparations were hurried forward so that the coronation of the new King should take place soon after daybreak.

There seemed nothing more for the Resident to do. He repaired to the verandah overhanging the Gumti, and there he sat, enjoying the cool dawn breezes and discussing plans with his assistants.

Suddenly news was brought to him that the Queen Begum, step-mother of the late King, was advancing upon the palace with a large armed band, intending to force the officials to crown a child called Moona Jan, either her illegitimate son or her adopted grandson, as King of Oudh.

Captain Paton, one of Colonel Low's assistants, at once rushed to the south gate, collecting four men as he ran, to find a seething mob already surging round the gate. The palace guards and the police had done nothing to disperse the mob who had already forced a passage. In poured the rabble, sweeping aside all resistance, even beating Captain Paton to the ground with lathis and musket butts. They spared his body servant who escaped out of the gate in time to bring an advance party of thirty sepoys to save his already insensible master's life from being beaten out of his body.

The rabble was by this time completely beyond control. Colonel Low was helpless and under the guard of a rebel sentry. He was forcibly taken to the Lal Baradari where the child Moona Jan was already seated upon the throne, listening to the state band playing, incongruously enough, a discordant version of 'God Save the King' !

The Resident and his assistants were dragged through the unruly crowd to the throne, where Colonel Low was peremptorily ordered to congratulate the young pretender. The penalty of refusal was, he was assured to the accompaniment of much brandishing of swords and daggers, instant death.

He refused, however, to show the least agitation. Quite calmly he represented to the Begum that even if she did kill him, the British Government would exact a large fine from her. She refused to listen, but her Vakil had sense enough to realise the truth of this assertion and to see that he and his mistress would suffer a heavy penalty if any British official were harmed. He took matters into his own hands. Grasping Colonel Low by the arm, he thrust a way through the muttering mob, shouting to all and sundry that by order of the Begum the Resident was to be escorted from the throne room. Even so, it was not an easy path. By dint of much pushing and elbowing they eventually reached the exit, accompanied by Captain Shakespeare, the second assistant. There in the garden they found five infantry companies and four guns which had just arrived from Mariaon under the command of Colonel Monteith. Colonel Low forthwith took command. He ordered the Begum and her youthful candidate to surrender, giving the old lady fifteen short minutes in which to disperse her followers. She still hoped against hope to triumph and would not obey. Colonel Low relinquished command of affairs to the soldiers. Then and there the guns opened fire upon the throne room while Major Marshall led a party of the 35th (Company's) Infantry to the attack, first firing upon the now panic-stricken people, then resorting to the bayonet.

The swashbuckling insurgents turned into cowering refugees, fleeing in wild disorder and leaving fifty of their number dead or wounded in the building. The British casualties were three or four wounded only.

The story goes that as the sepoys charged into the throne room they saw a number of wild-looking men advancing threateningly upon them from the opposite end of the hall. Not until they pened fire did they realise that they had mistaken for the enemy their own images reflected in a large mirror.

While these people of Oudh shed their blood in a futile cause, the dead body of their late king lay in state in one part of the palace, while the new king as yet uncrowned, sat, according to some authorities, cowering in fear of his life in an upper chamber of the palace, or according to others, sleeping peacefully throughout the proceedings. Ultimately the Begum and her protégé were captured and sent to Chunar as state prisoners. Nasir-ud-Doulah was finally crowned, upon which he changed his name to Muhammad Ali Shah. He proved worthy of the Government's choice, for he ruled as well and as wisely as his health would permit. To some extent he refilled the state coffers, sadly depleted almost to the last few rupees by the wanton extravagance of his predecessor.

The throne itself, so insecure for those who sat there, was of gold, embroidered in pearls and small rubies.

Some contemporary authorities held that he ought not to have succeeded to the throne, for Sa'adat Ali Khan had sons; and although his eldest son Shams-ud-Din died during his father's life-time, his four sons were not out of the line of succession. Their claims to the throne of Oudh were urged by Captain White in a pamphlet entitled 'The Prince of Oudh'. However that may be, Muhammad Ali Shah was the one ruler since his brother's death who tried to stem the tide of degeneracy which ultimately lost the line their kingdom.

Enfeebled and old though he was, he decided to beautify the Husainabad area of Lucknow. To that end he began building a structure known as the Sat Khanda which derived its name from the fact that it was designed to have seven storeys, from the topmost of which the King could lie on his couch and watch the progress of his building schemes. No more than five storeys were finished before he died. They stand incomplete to this day, gradually crumbling to decay in a corner of the Husainabad Park in which he built the Husainabad Tank, a graceful pool bordered at one end by another of his conceptions, the Taluqdars' Hall; also the florid, tawdry-looking Husainabad Imambara where he lies buried.

The Honourable Emily Eden, on a tour with her brother Lord Auckland, visited Lucknow in 1837. The King sent relays of coach horses to facilitate her approach to Lucknow and caused tents to be pitched for her comfort at convenient intervals along the route. The King's own cook also sallied forth to meet the party.

The Governor-General himself remained at Cawnpore, for etiquette did not permit the King, who was by this time bed-ridden, to receive a distinguished guest from his couch and without the pomp and ceremony which were a fitting accompaniment to the meeting of an Indian King with the British King's representative.

In 1837 a new treaty was drawn up by which Colonel Low hoped to guard against a repetition of such misrule as the former one, but it was never ratified as the Court of Directors for some reason did not approve of it.

Muhammad Ali Shah did his best to rule well, but it was a feeble and incapable best, for the poor old man was too broken in health to accomplish much. Hakim Mahdi was reinstated as minister but he died soon after he had resumed office. His successors, worthy men enough, lacked initiative to inaugurate a new system of government.

The King was popular and had a certain amount of influence over his subjects, especially as he made determined efforts to improve the city and did not dispense all thought and substance upon his own palace. He spent large sums in making Husainabad a broad and handsome street. When he died his treasury contained about £800,000. This was substantial enough, taking into consideration his extensive building operations and the fact that he had succeeded to a bare pittance.

Prince Alexis Soltikoff visited Lucknow at the close of 1841 and describes Husainabad as a large and noisy street, terminated by a gateway of Moorish design, behind which towered slender minarets with small golden domes gleaming in the sun. At one end of the broad highway stood the Imambara, enclosing aviaries of rare and lovely birds, several edifices of Eastern design, and a small gilded mosque erected over the remains of the queen mother.

Only a few months later, in May 1842, the King himself was laid to rest in a silver sarcophagus, to be succeeded by his second son.

AMJAD ALI SHAH
1842—1847

KING AMJAD ALI SHAH WAS the second son of his predecessor Muhammad Ali Shah. His elder brother Ashar Ali died young so that his son Mumtaz-ud-Doulah, formerly in direct succession, was thenceforward of no account.

It was already May when the old King died, but undeterred by the heat of the summer, Amjad Ali Shah gave full rein to excess and vice. All reforms attempted by his father were nullified. The country went from bad to worse. Almost the only good things he seems to have done were to erect the Iron Bridge over the Gumti, which had been lying by the wayside for more than thirty years, and to construct the road to Cawnpore which still follows the same route. His minister Amin-ud-Doulah built the great Aminabad bazar and *serai* on the Cawnpore Road, now engulfed in the heart of Lucknow city.

The King also built his own mausoleum and the street of Hazrat Ganj, in which it now lies forgotten and deserted, given over to rats, cobwebs and decay.

Von Orlich visited Lucknow soon after Amjad Ali Shah's accession and was granted audience by the King in the Farhat Bakhsh. General Nott was the new Resident and was assisted by Captain Shakespeare who had been one of the actors in the tumultuous scene at Muhammad Ali Shah's accession.

The Resident presented Von Orlich to the King, who impressed the visitor as being tall, rather fat, benevolent-looking, but extremely ugly, having an enormous nose. On this occasion he wore a robe of green silk lavishly embroidered with gold and silver threads, which opened to disclose red silk pantaloons and gold embroidered shoes. Upon his head he wore a high jewelled cap. Round his neck and upon his fingers flashed priceless jewels.

Amjad Ali Shah is always depicted as wearing the most gorgeous robes and jewels. Not one costly chain but four hung round his neck; a magnificent osprey surmounted his crown, which blazed with jewels. In the palace a special table was reserved for a large assortment of head-dresses for it pleased the King to change these at frequent intervals.

At the end of an interview the chamberlain produced the golden embroidered garlands for which Lucknow is still justly famed. The royal ones were made of silver thread and incorporated the kingly arms of two swords, a tiara, a crown, and the famous fish emblem embossed in gold upon silver shields. These garlands the King with his own hand placed around the necks of his visitors before escorting them to the entrance of the palace. There he was wont to embrace them, shake them warmly by the hand and retire.

King Amjad Ali Shah cared nothing for manly sports. Instead, he passed a great deal of his time in his harem where dwelt a very remarkable woman, his chief wife, daughter of Hasin-ud-Din, Khan of Kalpi. Hers were not the only attractions which drew the King so often to the women's quarters of the palace. He had nearly two hundred concubines. His eldest son thus had the worst possible upbringing for one of his inherited tendencies.

This King cared nothing for affairs of state and took no interest in the government of his country in spite of repeated representations from the British Resident that if he did not mend his ways of his own accord, steps would be taken by the Governor-General to see that he was made to do so.

In 1845 Sir Henry Lawrence paid a tribute to these kings. He said: "The Oudh rulers have been no worse than monarchs so situated usually are; indeed, they have been better than might have been expected. Weak, vicious, and dissolute they were, but they have seldom been cruel, and have never been false. In the storms of the last half century, Oudh is the one single native state that has invariably been true to the British Government: that has neither intrigued against us nor seemed to desire our injury."

The verdict of so stern a moralist should be remembered by those who are inclined to think of all the Kings of Oudh alike as monsters of treachery and misrule.

WAJID ALI SHAH
1847–1856

WAJID ALI SHAH SUCCEEDED TO the throne of Oudh on February 14, 1847, on the death of his father Amjad Ali Shah who made a deathbed prophecy that the country would never prosper under his son's rule. Wajid Ali Shah was not the eldest son, but his elder brother had already been disqualified as feeble-minded and incurably vice-ridden.

Wajid Ali was reputed to be neither stupid nor unamiable. He had won a place in literature, and some reputation both as poet and writer of prose. It was unfortunate that the happiness of millions depended upon him.

His chief wife was Khas Mahal, niece of the minister Nawab Naqi Khan and mother of the heir-apparent. In addition he owned three other wives, four hundred concubines, and twenty-nine *muta* wives. *Muta* is a sort of inferior marriage amongst Mussalmans which may be binding for three hours, three days, three months, or three years. To house this enormous harem, he built the Kaiser Bagh, "the largest, gaudiest and most debased of all the Lucknow palaces," at the fabulous cost of about eighty lakhs of rupees. He was known to have had at least forty-five sons and thirty-four daughters who also resided there. Each woman had her own suite of rooms and her own attendants. It was whispered that the King's chief consort was a profligate woman.

He passed much of his time in his harem amongst the nautch girls who were "celebrated for their sociability and education, the generality of them possessing a colloquial knowledge of Persian".

Rumour had it that the rapid demise of former kings of Oudh had been due to the bite of a snake concealed within the cushions of the throne, so Wajid Ali refused to sit thereon. He contented himself with touching the throne seven times, bowing the while. Local legend said that this throne was the very one used by King Solomon himself.

Wajid Ali Shah possessed histrionic ability but it took the form of a preference for portraying female parts. He always took the chief part in a play which was annually enacted in the silver baradari at the Kaiser Bagh. During festivals, too, he would seat himself cross-legged at the base of a sacred mulberry tree and receive the petitions of his humble subjects who would otherwise have no access to the royal ear. When giving audience, however, he saw himself more as a literary character than as a kingly redresser of wrongs and no material good came of these personal contacts.

Wajid Ali was hypochondriacal, but he refused to consult the Residency surgeon, preferring the medical advice of every sort of quack and witch doctor. One in particular, hearing that the King was suffering from palpitations of the heart, came to Lucknow in the guise of a dervish and took up his residence in the Muftee Ganj quarter. Here he gave himself out to be one of the Kings of the Fairies. He was soon able to extort large sums of money from the King on a false promise of being able to cure him.

Sleeman held strong views on the subject. He said that the King was totally unfit to govern and, moreover, took not the faintest interest in the welfare of his country. He cared only for singing and dancing and for those versed in such arts, be they of ever such humble origin. He brooked no interference, would receive no one but those low caste, lewd entertainers, and insisted that his sons be brought up in the same disgusting debauchery. The consequence was that the whole country despised and hated him. All his substance he squandered upon his low friends, who fleeced him right and left. He commanded that they be treated with all pomp and ceremony wherever they chose to go.

The administration of the kingdom was given over to the Taluqdars who, unqualified to deal with the sudden access of authority, heartily abused their position of trust. Matters reached such a pitch that finally Wajid Ali received a letter from the Governor-General saying that it had been decided to effect the formal annexation of Oudh to British territory. Wajid Ali was stunned by the news and sat alone weeping. His mother was closeted with him for many hours in conference. During the afternoon the English Resident visited him for another long parley at which the Queen was present. In the evening soldiers came into Lucknow from the Cantonment across the river, cannons were removed from the palaces, and the English *raj* began.

Lord Dalhousie, the Governor-General, offered to let Wajid Ali Shah and his successors retain the title and dignity of king, and to enjoy sovereign rights within the Palace at Lucknow and the Bibiapur and Dilkusha Parks ; but Wajid Ali refused to accept this or to sign any treaty, saying that treaties were necessary only between equals, and that he was in no position to sign one. He debased himself by uncovering his head and placing his turban in the hands of the Resident, declaring that he himself was now as nothing. On February 7, General Outram formally annexed the kingdom on behalf of the East India Company. The King left Lucknow on March 13, arriving in Calcutta two months later, having taken with him as many jewels and valuables as he could carry away from Lucknow. In Calcutta he occupied the house and grounds at Garden Reach formerly inhabited by Sir Lawrence Peel, Chief Justice of the Supreme Court from 1848 to 1855. During the troubles of 1857 the ex-King was arrested merely by way of a precaution and detained in Fort William, Calcutta, as a state prisoner until July, 1859.

About seventeen years later a visitor described how the ex-King's estate was thrown open to visitors on New Year's Day. He had a pitiable menagerie of neglected, ill-fed tigers, buffaloes, snakes and birds. Guarding the entrance to the house stood sepoys, still clad in obsolete uniforms which they had worn since the days of splendour at Lucknow.

Wajid Ali continued to be terribly extravagant. He was a curious mixture and latterly divided his time between religious observances and his menagerie. On one occasion a pair of vultures took the ex-King's fancy. Their price, he was told, was Rs. 50,000. Nothing daunted, he insisted upon purchasing them in spite of the fact that the treasury contained only Rs. 35,000. To make up the difference he ordered that one of the two golden bedsteads made during the reign of the great Sa'adat Ali Khan should be broken up, melted down, and the balance paid.

The ex-King's pension amounted to a lakh of rupees a month, then worth about £120,000 a year. He lived in Calcutta until he died, at the age of sixty-seven, on September 21, 1887.

THE RESIDENCY

THE TERM "RESIDENCY" NOW includes a large protected enclosure. Originally it applied only to the large English-looking house, colour-washed in yellow, conceived for the British Residency by Nawab Asaf-ud-Doulah in 1780 and finished by Nawab Sa'adat Ali Khan twenty years later.

The house stands upon what was then the highest point of Lucknow. It boasted three storeys. At one corner a tower projected a foot or two above the roof, bearing the flagstaff from which generations of Union Jacks have proudly waved. Wide verandahs shielded the interior from the sun. Beneath still lies a suite of *tykhanas*, or underground rooms, which remain dark and cool in the glare of the hottest summer day, although the narrow slits in the upper walls admit of but scant ventilation.

Until Captain John Baillie became Resident at the beginning of the nineteenth century there was no guard over the house. He, however, soon protested against this shortcoming, with the result that the Nawab built a guard house, now famous as the Baillie Gate, to be occupied by a company from Mariaon, five miles across the river.

The Marquess of Hastings records that he dined with Major Baillie at the Residency in 1814. Later the road led up the slope through some folding gates into a close, surrounded by gardens and well built houses, with barracks at the entrance. One of these houses was occupied by the Resident ; another was his banqueting hall, containing apartments for his guests ; a third was unusually pleasing and assigned to guests of the King of Oudh. Stables for horses and adequate accommodation for 'a brave retinue' were accompanying features of this third house.

For another thirty years, until the outbreak of 1857, the community clustered about these delightful buildings on the little hill, unheeding the fate in store for them.

A brief knowledge of the events of the Mutiny is essential to appreciate the ruins of the historic enclosure. Things began to move imperceptibly many months before the actual outbreak. The first tangible evidence of the Mutiny in Lucknow was on May 2, when the 7th Oudh Irregulars at the Moosa Bagh refused to bite the new cartridge. After that incident the rebels became ever braver until their sense of superiority was complete.

The events of the siege proper could not be better summed up than in the words set upon a tablet on the wall of the women's quarters, above the *tykhanas* of the Residency.

"On 30th June, 1857 A.D., the day after the battle of Chinhut, the siege began. On the 2nd July, Sir Henry Lawrence was mortally wounded by a shell which burst within the Residency building. The command then devolved on Brigadier J. E. W. Inglis of Her Majesty's 32nd Regiment. The force within the defence then consisted of 130 officers, British and native, 74 British and 700 native troops and 150 civilian volunteers. There were 237 women, 260 children, 50 boys of La Martinière College, 27 non-combatant Europeans and 700 non-combatant natives, being a total of 2,994 souls. From the 30th June to the 25th September, for eighty-seven days, they were closely invested, subjected to a heavy artillery fire, day and night, on all sides, and had to sustain several general attacks on the position. On the 25th September, 1857 A.D., Generals Outram and Havelock, with a large force, endeavoured to release the garrison, after having, with great loss, effected a juncture with them. They were, however, unable to withdraw, and the whole combined force was besieged for a period of fifty-three days, until finally relieved by Sir Colin Campbell on the 17th November, 1857 A.D. There remained of the original garrison, when relieved on the 25th September, a total of 979 souls, including sick and wounded, of whom 577 were European and 402 natives."

So emaciated and weakened was every living thing within the Residency that those camels and horses which had survived when the time came for the final exodus found it scarcely possible to drag one limb after the other.

The first night of freedom was spent at the Secunder Bagh, the weak refugees starting fearfully at every untoward sound. The following day, on crept the pitiful train to Dilkusha, 'Heart's Delight'. For these hearts which had suffered so much in those few short months, there can have been little delight.

THE BAILLIE GUARD GATEWAY from which the gate has long since disappeared was, during the siege, effectively banked with earth and sandbags from the inside. To the right a battery of two nine-pounders and an eight-inch howitzer defended the entrance. On September 25, Havelock at the head of his relieving force reached the famous gateway as darkness fell to find the barricade impassable owing to its fortifications. A gun thrust through a breach was hastily withdrawn, and the troops marched in, Havelock and Outram riding at their head, to receive a welcome that only those who were present could ever fully appreciate. An hour or two later despair fell deeper by sharp contrast, when the beleaguered garrison realised that the force was no relief at all but an added burden, requiring food, accommodation and ammunition, all of which were already at a premium.

As Havelock's force streamed through the breach, men of his troops, their blood heated to fever point from fighting every inch of their way through the streets of Lucknow, bayoneted by mistake three of the sepoys belonging to the 13th Native Infantry. "*Kuch parwa nahin, Kismet hai ..Baillie Guard ki jai,*" they said. "Never mind. It was fate. Victory to the Baillie Guard." Although these men had been within speaking distance of the enemy throughout the siege, no threats or cajolements could persuade them to desert. Lord Canning wrote: "Their courageous constancy under the severest trials is worthy of all honour." After the Mutiny the three faithful regiments, the 13th, 48th and 71st Native Infantry Regiments were formed into the 16th (Lucknow) Rajput Regiment.

THE TREASURY stands immediately on the right of the Baillie Guard entrance, the long centre room being commandeered during the siege for the manufacture of Enfield cartridges. Lieut. Aitken commanded the garrison composed of detachments from the 13th and 48th Native Infantry Regiments, to the former of which he belonged. He was assisted by Loughman with whose help they constructed and manned an eighteen-pounder gun. It is recorded that he commanded the sepoys "with signal courage and success". They had also to garrison the Baillie Gate, holding it against great odds in the assault on July 20. Lieut. Aitken gained the V.C. for various acts of gallantry at Lucknow. Some years later he became Inspector-General of Police in Oudh.

Just above the Treasury is the BANQUETING HALL, also under the command of Lieut. Aitken during the siege. Originally it served the double purpose of Banqueting Hall and Council Chamber. Above the Resident's offices on the ground floor were luxuriously furnished apartments reserved as guest rooms. The building made an admirable hospital. One room, on the north side, was set apart for state prisoners, including Mustafa Ali Khan, a brother of the ex-King of Oudh, the Rajah of Tulsipore and two princes related to the Emperor of Delhi. One of the latter, Nawab Nakun-un-Doulah, died during the siege. He was buried at the gate of Ommaney's post opposite the front entrance to the Residency proper. The enemy knew, through spies, that prisoners were kept in this building and forbore to fire heavily upon it. Here the Reverend Henry Polehampton, during his ceaseless tending of the sick, was severely wounded on July 8. His devotion was such that "he never swerved from this self-imposed duty and only left the hospital to go to his meals." He was well on the road to recovery after his wound when he contracted cholera. He died less than a fortnight later. Towards the end of June, he and his wife had moved into a small room in the hospital building where Mrs. Polehampton busied herself with the sick.

DR. FAYRER'S HOUSE stands across the road opposite to the Banqueting Hall. Dr. Fayrer was the Residency surgeon at the time of the Mutiny and showed all the kindness in his power to the poor refugees who crowded into the Residency at the order of Sir Henry Lawrence. Dr. and Mrs. Fayrer were a young couple who had a beautiful baby boy. At the beginning of the siege he was eleven months' old, and the plaything of all the inmates of the house. By the beginning of August, through lack of good nourishment, poor little Bobby Fayrer was very ill. Never had there been such a sad change in any baby. From being a "lovely cherub of a child" he had shrunk to mere skin and bones and looked like a little wizened old man.

For the women, cooped up in the house, life was extremely monotonous. Each day they rose at four o'clock and sat in front of the house, where they drank a little tea and ate biscuits while such delicacies lasted. At eight o'clock they went indoors and busied themselves with setting their rooms in order. They would then put the finishing touches to their toilet before reading the Psalms and Lessons of the day, and praying. Breakfast was at ten. The rest of the morning they would sit together in the drawing-room, where the temperature was about ninety-three, sewing or playing with the children. They dined at four. When the sun set they emerged from the sheltering stone walls to have tea and ices. Prayers were again said at nine-thirty. After that they went to bed in stuffy little rooms even hotter than the drawing-room. The only change or excitement was in the shape of bad news or horrible alarms.

Many of them slept together in the *tykhana* where they spread mattresses on the floor, lying cheek by jowl so as to reap the maximum benefit from the punkah. The room had nothing but skylights, so they ate their meals by the fitful light of a candle. The normal fare was stew "as being easiest to cook ; it is brought up in a large *deckgee* so as not to dirty a dish, and a portion ladled out to each person. Of course, we can get no bread or butter, so *chupattis* are the disagreeable substitute. Two eighteen-pounders came through the room Emmie and I used to sleep in, and where we have since always gone to perform an alarmed and hurried toilet. We dress now in a tiny barricaded closet out of the dining-room where no balls have come yet. We are all going to sleep in the dining-room to-night. The *tykhana* is too damp, everyone is ill and the dining-room is *tolerably* safe." Mercifully, the summer of 1857 proved a remarkably mild one. Instead of the relentless succession of days of burning sun, sullen clouds shielded the earth from unbearable heat.

When Sir Henry Lawrence was wounded he was removed to Dr. Fayrer's house where Mrs. Harris, wife of one of the clergymen, stayed upstairs all day to nurse him. He lingered for a day or two in extreme suffering, for "his screams are so terrible I think the sound will never leave my ears." He died at a quarter past eight on the morning of July 4.

The Fayrers' house was built on sloping ground so that on the Residency side it had but one storey and on the city side two. Captain Weston of the Oudh Police defended it with sepoy pensioners, for its flat roof encircled by sandbags afforded a point of vantage for sharp-shooters. Below was a battery of brass nine-pounder howitzers and an eighteen-pounder gun.

SANDERS' POST was originally the Financial Commissioner's office, and was a big double-storeyed house manned by men of the 32nd under Captain Sanders of the 13th Native Infantry.

SAGO'S HOUSE was another of the front line defence posts which, owing to its salient position, was particularly vulnerable. It was a small one-storeyed building exposed on three sides to the enemy, and formerly belonged to a school mistress, Mrs. Sago. During the siege this house was garrisoned by a party of the 32nd under Lieut. Clery.

GERMON'S POST was within a stone's throw of Sago's House. Transit from one to the other was down a narrow passage and was fraught with much danger. Formerly the Judicial Commissioner's office, it was commanded by Captain Germon of the 13th Native Infantry and garrisoned by some of his own Sikhs and by uncovenanted civilians. It was a big two-storeyed house which sheltered the families of the uncovenanted civilians. So near were besieged and besiegers that instead of bullets rounds of abuse were often exchanged which may account for the fact that several feet of the walls are still standing.

THE POST OFFICE lay behind and to one side of Germon's Post, and on slightly higher ground. In front of it were placed a couple of mortars and four guns. Now only a pillar remains to mark the position of what was then a building housing a large number of European soldiers and several families. It was an important defence post, an officer constantly remaining on watch upon the roof. The gallant Captain Barnard McCabe of His Majesty's 32nd Regiment was in command, although the position was the headquarters of both the Royal Engineers and the Artillery. Captain McCabe was mortally wounded when leading his fourth sortie. He died on October 4.

THE THUG GAOL was a long narrow building in the second line of defence, in the cells of which many women and children were housed. Some thirty years before the Mutiny, the Hon. Emily Eden noted in her diary that on her flying visit to Lucknow she was taken for a hurried look at the Thug Gaol.

ANDERSON'S POST was a small double-storeyed house lying upon a slope in what was one of the most exposed positions of the entrenchment. By the middle of July the brick-work had been entirely shot away. Throughout the siege the enemy was never more than forty yards away, keeping up an incessant fusillade.

Captain Anderson of the 25th Native Infantry commanded it with a small garrison of nine privates and a sergeant of the 32nd, a subaltern, and eight volunteers, amongst whom was an Italian Signor Barsetelli whose unending sense of humour played no small part in keeping up the courage of his fellows.

THE CAWNPORE BATTERY, hard by Anderson's Post, consisted of three field guns, but it was such a dangerous position that the garrison was relieved every day by a Captain and detachment of the 32nd. It commanded a wide area of hostile ground, including two main roads of strategic importance.

DUPRAT'S HOUSE was in an open position next to the Cawnpore Battery. Its owner, M. Duprat, was a Frenchman who had come from Calcutta to set up as a merchant, and who became known as a gallant soldier, as well as a popular member of the garrison. He succumbed to a wound in the face during August.

THE MARTINIERE POST was a strongly built house. Underneath it were *tykhanas* and adjoining it outhouses, the property of an Indian banker named Shah Bihari Lall. It was only thirty feet distant from Johannes House, a point in possession of the enemy. The Martinière Post was garrisoned by a detachment of the 32nd Regiment, the masters, and about fifty of the bigger boys of the Martinière College, under the command of Mr. George Schilling, Principal of the College. The smaller boys, of whom there were about fifteen, were told off to run messages to the hospital, etc., during hostilities. They proved willing little helpers. Surprisingly, only three boys were wounded during the entire siege, and two died of disease.

The Native Hospital lay behind the Martinière Post which protected it from the enemy's fire. A mortar was near by.

The King's Hospital, a little further on, was in the front line of defence. Later, during hostilities, it was known as the Brigade Mess. Here were quartered the officers of regiments which had mutinied. Here also lived Mrs. (afterwards Lady) Couper, wife of Sir Henry Lawrence's secretary, in a room some ten feet square, with many other women and children. The building, solid and spacious, gave a good view of the city from the roof. Colonel Master of the 7th Light Cavalry got his nickname of "The Admiral" owing to his habit of hailing from the roof top. The officers found this roof a good vantage point for sniping. It was largely owing to their good marksmanship that the enemy attacks on August 11 and 18 failed. Known to be a dangerous post, the enemy rained bullets into it on every occasion until, by the end of August, the upper part had become a mere ruin. On September 7 two hundred and eighty round shots were collected from it, varying in size from a twenty-four pounder to a three-pounder. At the back were the Brigadier's quarters and those of Lady Inglis and her children.

Johannes House stood exactly opposite to the Brigade Mess, but outside the line of defences. Previous to the outbreak of hostilities Johannes, an Armenian, was the richest merchant in Lucknow. It had been intended to include his house within the Residency area, but so swift was the debacle after the battle of Chinhut that the enemy occupied it before the British could do so. The Armenian's house remained a constant source of trouble until August 12 when a cunningly placed mine exploded and the whole building tumbled to ruins, dragging with it a number of mutineers. Chief amongst its garrison was an African, formerly in the army of the King of Oudh, whom the defenders nicknamed "Bob the Nailer", for his aim was so accurate that every shot he fired literally "nailed" his man.

THE SIKH SQUARE consisted of two quadrangular courtyards surrounded by low flat-roofed buildings and a horse picket yard for fifty cavalry and artillery horses. It adjoined the Brigade Mess and was garrisoned by the Sikh Cavalry and some Christian drummers under the command of Captain Hardinge of the Oudh Irregular Cavalry and other officers who were relieved in weekly rotation. The loyalty of the Sikhs was a much debated question, but the majority of them remained staunch and proved invaluable as miners. For this hazardous work each man was paid at the rate of two rupees a day.

THE BEGUM'S HOUSE behind the horse-lines of Sikh Square was a large building on the roof of which the two minarets and three domes of a small mosque still stand. The house was the dwelling of a Mrs. Walters and her elder daughter who was known as Begum Ashraf-ul-Nisa. The younger daughter, under the title of Mukhaddar-i-Ulaya, had married King Nasir-ud-Din Haider, who reigned from 1827 to 1837.

OMMANNEY'S HOUSE stood close to the Begum's House some way back from the front line fortified in case the troops should have occasion to fall back upon it.

GRANT'S BASTION occupied a prominent position, separated from Sikh Square by a long narrow passage in possession of the enemy, at the blind end of which stood a British mortar,

GUBBINS' BATTERY was an outwork which protected the south-west corner of the position, and was garrisoned by covenanted civilians. Many of their names have since become famous, such as Ommanney, Couper, Martin, Capper Thornhill and Lawrence.

GUBBINS' HOUSE stood not far from Gubbins' Battery, but scarcely anything except the swimming bath remains of what was once a large house with an imposing front portico. Water was plentiful throughout the siege, and this swimming bath was a great boon. At first the house was filled to overflowing with ladies and children occupying the upper storey, but towards the end of August it became unsafe from the number of round shot poured into it by the enemy, so all but the garrison vacated it. Details of the 32nd, the 48th Native Infantry, Pensioners and Gubbins' Levies comprised the garrison under Major Banks, Captain Forbes, 1st Light Infantry, Captain Hawes, 5th Oudh Irregular Infantry, and finally under Major Apthorpe, 41st Native Infantry. Major Banks was mortally wounded at this post, also Captain Fulton of the Engineers, who by general consent was accorded the palm of merit for his conduct during the defence. Mr. Gubbins was financial secretary of Oudh and he afterwards wrote an illuminating book about the siege.

THE SLAUGHTER-HOUSE POST lay along part of the west wall of the defences. It is now only marked by pillars, but originally consisted of outhouses belonging to the Residency, including a sheep pen and a slaughter-house. They were held by uncovenanted civilians under Captain Boileau of the 7th Light Cavalry. Nearly every officer who slept there contracted fever owing to the unwholesome and overpowering stench which arose from the decaying entrails of the butcher's daily victims. These were simply thrown over the parapet as the only means of disposing of them.

St. Mary's Church, a handsome Gothic building, had been erected in 1810. Well shaded by trees and surrounded by a wall, it had no churchyard for the good reason that India did not bury her dead near churches in those days. The east window was an imitation, likewise the side aisles which were verandahs where stood the punkah coolies. The church held a hundred and thirty people. The first to be buried in the church garden were the victims of the surprise attack upon Mariaon. During the siege, the church, standing on a slope, was very exposed. In spite of this, services were regularly held. Artillery horses were picketed in the garden, and stores stowed away in part of the building itself. The vestry and other shelters housed refugees, giving the church a most warlike appearance. At one time the authorities seriously considered blowing it up. The idea, however, was abandoned because it involved the useless expenditure of gunpowder.

Burials were conducted under cover of darkness by two gallant padres, Harris and Polehampton. It was impossible to dig very deep, partly owing to the time factor, and the bodies were merely wrapped in sheets and laid in the ground, with the result that the churchyard developed a most offensive smell, making the wretched clergymen ill. Polehampton died from cholera contracted while convalescing from the effects of a severe wound. His young wife, who had but lately lost her only child, was anxious that her husband should have a coffin, a simple wish that seemed impossible to gratify, for wood was at a premium. A search was made, however, and an old coffin found, stowed away with some boxes under a staircase at the hospital. He was duly buried in a separate grave. During the siege those who died were normally sewn up in their bedding and buried in one grave.

The death of the brave clergyman was a serious loss, for he had been unremitting in his kindness to the sick and wounded in the hospital. He never swerved from a self-imposed duty, and only left the hospital to go to his meals.

Innes House stood on an exposed peninsula of ground below the church, and separated from it by a low mud-wall. It was originally occupied by Lieut. James McLeod Innes of the Bengal Engineers. During the Mutiny a party of the 32nd Regiment defended it, augmented by a handful of sepoys of the 13th Native Infantry, and by some uncovenanted civilians, all under the command of Lieut. Longman of the 13th Native Infantry and later of Captain Craydon of the 44th Native Infantry. The house itself was large and well-built, with a sloping roof and verandahs on two sides. An inside staircase led to the roof. In one corner of the compound stood a small double-storeyed shed, the upper floor being known during the siege as the cockloft, commanding a view of the Iron Bridge spanning the Gumti.

On July 20, a massed attack was launched against the Residency with Innes House as its primary objective. The enemy came within ten yards of the stockade carrying scaling ladders, but met with such a hot reception that they were forced to retire as attack after attack repeatedly failed. They nearly succeeded, however, in occupying the cockloft. Mr. Ereth, a corporal in the Volunteers, rushed forward through a hail of bullets only to fall mortally wounded in the neck. He was a railway contractor who had been married a bare three months. Such was his self-effacement and keenness that when he lay dying in hospital, he asked whether all was going well at Innes Post. No sooner had he fallen than Mr. George Bailey, another volunteer, doubled up with a few sepoys who succeeded in holding their own in spite of being badly wounded.

The insurgents continued to make isolated attacks on the various outposts during the whole morning, but contented themselves in the latter part of the day with heavy musketry and gun fire. At the diagonally opposite corner of Innes' enclosure a rebel standard-bearer was actually shot in the ditch of the Cawnpore Battery, so close had he advanced. In spite of fierce fighting the British losses were only four killed and twelve wounded. Lady Inglis records that "this attack and its complete repulse raised all our spirits and gave us confidence that with God's help we should be able to hold out till succour arrived. It was the severest assault that the enemy had yet made, and John said the bullets fell like hail."

THE REDAN BATTERY stood not far from the Water Gate. It was built during June by Captain Fulton, a Sapper, and a very gallant man. He discovered some Cornish miners in the ranks of the 32nd, and with them conducted all the mining of the siege. There is in Lucknow a picture of him crouched in a mine, revolver in hand, like a terrier at a rat-hole. He was wonderfully brave, and took great risks with supreme modesty. He was killed on

September 14 by a round shot, having won from his comrades the title of "The Defender of Lucknow."

The Redan Battery was the strongest within the defences, having two eighteen-pounders and one nine-pounder with which to rake the riverside. It was manned by men of the 32nd Regiment under one of their own officers, Lieut. Sam Lawrence. Here it was that Mr. Ommanney, the Judicial Commissioner, was fatally wounded by a cannon ball which struck his head. Two enemy attempts were made to blow up the battery, but in vain.

THE ALAM BAGH

COMPARED WITH MANY OF THE historic buildings in and around Lucknow, the Alam Bagh on the Cawnpore Road is relatively modern, for it was built by Wajid Ali Shah, the last King of Oudh, who reigned from 1847 to 1856. It was built as a country residence for one of his favourite wives, but it is hard to realise that a pleasant garden once covered the dreary waste now surrounding the ruins of a compact house. Each of the four corners is ornamented by an octagonal tower, on one of which a semaphore post established the only means of communication with the beleaguered garrison in the Residency in 1857. The house consists of two storeys, and there is not a single window in the entire building. A battered brick wall surrounds the erstwhile garden, and both it and the solid square entrance gate still show great holes where the enemy made repeated attacks upon the gallant little force pressing on to relieve their comrades pent up in the Residency.

On July 7, 1857 Havelock proceeded with a small force of 1,400 British and 550 Indians to the relief of Lucknow. An Indian pensioner named Ungud got through the besieging force several times, carrying letters from Brigadier Inglis (who by that time was in command at the Residency owing to the death of Sir Henry Lawrence) to Sir Henry Havelock at the Alam Bagh. On July 25, Havelock sent Ungud back to the Residency with a letter saying, "We have two-thirds of our force across the river, and eight guns in position already. The rest will follow immediately. We have ample force to destroy all who oppose us......" This struck an unduly optimistic note and after five great actions had been fought and won, Havelock's losses were so severe that he decided to fall back to Cawnpore on August 17. Havelock was then superseded by Sir James Outram. The country people said of him: "A fox is a fool and a lion is a coward by the side of Outram Sahib."

On September 23, the column again sighted the Alam Bagh but found it strongly held by about 10,000 trained sepoys and many guns. From there, crossing the Cawnpore Road and extending for some two miles, stretched a line of hostile troops, the centre upon rising ground and the right flank lying behind a marshy swamp. The rebels had concentrated the bulk of their troops in the Alam Bagh and were taken completely by surprise when Havelock sent his second Brigade through the heavy marsh land. Eyre's heavy battery crashed up the road, while Major Olpherts' battery galloped along to cover the advance of the 2nd Brigade, amid the cheers of the 1st Brigade. Soon they had to leave the road and cross a deep ditch filled with water. The cavalry escort crossed it without much difficulty and halted for the guns. "Hell-Fire Jack" Olpherts was not to be beaten.

For a moment there was chaos: a wild medley of detachments, drivers, guns, struggling horses and splashing water; and then the guns were on the further side, nobody and nothing the worse for the scramble, all hands on the alert to obey Olpherts' shout, "Forward, gallop." The enemy, taken by surprise, fled in confusion and the force attacking the Alam Bagh, reinforced by the 5th Fusiliers on the south side and the 78th at the main entrance, carried it with a rush. A Malacca cane was Outram's only weapon and brandishing it he led the pursuit of the enemy for several miles. That night news was received of the fall of Delhi, which raised still higher the soldiers' spirits, although afterwards the report was found to be erroneous.

The next move was to be *via* the Sikandra Bagh to the Residency, leaving Major McIntyre of the 78th at Alam Bagh, in charge of 280 European soldiers, a few Sikhs, four guns, about 130 sick and wounded, some 4,000 native followers, the baggage, the reserve food, and the ammunition. Although they fought no actual engagement, the rebel cavalry was always skirmishing round and it was a relief when on October 7 a reinforcement arrived from Cawnpore consisting of two hundred men and two guns, and later on five hundred infantry, fifty cavalry and two more guns appeared. On November 6, the sick and wounded were removed to Cawnpore under the escort of a strong force.

Four days later Kavanagh made his famous journey out of the Residency to the Alam Bagh thereby gaining the Victoria Cross. Although his wife and children were in the Residency, he volunteered to make his way out in disguise in order to guide the relieving force. Brigadier Inglis refused to allow him to go unless his disguise was impenetrable. Accordingly he dressed himself as an Indian, and walked boldly into the officers' dining-room in the Residency, where he sat down uninvited and without removing his shoes—in those days two dreadful breaches of etiquette. The officers remonstrated with him for several minutes, but until he revealed himself they did not penetrate his disguise. So he made for the river by way of the entrenchments, swam across and recrossed again by the old stone bridge. Then he walked boldly through the heart of the city full of rebel posts and finally reached the Alam Bagh. On November 12, the force encamped there was joined by more troops from Cawnpore, and at 9 a.m. on the 14th, the march towards the Residency began by way of Dilkusha and La Martinière.

On November 17, the relieving force made its way into the Residency, and before them all, untouched by the hail of bullets, ran Kavanagh. Not until his safe return was his wife told of his gallant exploit. A link with Kavanagh was severed in 1934 by the death in England of Mrs. Long, his daughter, who went through the siege at the age of eight.

She was twice married, her second husband having been in the 10th Royal Hussars. Her sister who also endured the siege was still alive at that date.

On November 18, Sir Colin Campbell decided to evacuate the Residency and to leave a strong force near the Alam Bagh. Two days later Havelock fell ill and died on November 24 in a soldier's tent in the garden of Dilkusha. The next day his remains were taken to the Alam Bagh, and buried there in the presence of the Commander-in-Chief and many officers and men.

Pending the erection of a monument, the letter "H" was cut, it is said, by Outram himself in a mango tree whose branches shaded the grave. An obelisk has since been erected there bearing his proud record, and in 1897 was added a memorial to his son, Lieutenant-General Sir Henry Marshman Havelock Allen, Bt., V.C., who was killed by Afridis in the Khyber Pass.

In the same peaceful little graveyard, amongst sweet-smelling flowering shrubs, lie the remains of several other officers and men who gave their lives in those troublous years of 1857 and 1858.

THE BADSHAH BAGH

KING NASIR-UD-DIN HAIDER, about a hundred years ago, built himself a high-walled garden which he called the Badshah Bagh. In the centre of pleasant walks was an open hall supported by fine carved pillars, where were held the festive gatherings of the period. Between the formal walks, gaily-hued flowers bordered shallow marble lakes filled with sweet-scented rose water, in which the favourites of the harem were wont to disport themselves.

The King is reputed to have included European beauties in his harem. For them he built the Walaiti Bagh. Within the Badshah Bagh he caused a square house washed in red ochre to be erected for their convenience. Thither also the nobility and leaders of fashion would repair to witness cock-fights, famous through Zoffany's painting of "Colonel Mordaunt's Cock Fight" in which many notables of the day may be recognised, including Zoffany himself holding a paint brush.

In November 1857, when the second relief force under Sir Colin Campbell had advanced to within a few hundred yards of their objective, the enemy made one last attempt to prevent the British from crossing the river, raking the troops with a heavy fire from the Kaisar Bagh in front and from the Badshah Bagh behind. A few months later, in March 1858, the British erected a battery at the south-west corner near the river to bombard the Kaisar Bagh whose inhabitants still clung to a forlorn hope.

Soon afterwards the Badshah Bagh became the property of the Maharajah of Kapurthala. In the garden stands a stone cross beneath which lie the remains of the eldest son of one of the Maharajahs. He became a Christian and thereby forfeited the right both to succeed to the throne and to be gathered unto his fathers when death befell him.

On May 1, 1864, a high school was opened in the Aminabad Palace, attended by over two hundred boys. The Taluqdars of Oudh guaranteed to contribute Rs. 25,000 annually towards its upkeep provided the Government did the same. Two years later it was raised to the status of a College, known as the Canning College. In 1867 it was affiliated to the Calcutta University for the Bachelor of Arts Degree and for Law in 1870. Later it was affiliated to the Allahabad University. At one period the College was housed in a building within the Kaisar Bagh, once the seat of Government and now a museum housing stone carvings, belonging to the Government of the United Provinces. At present the building is used by the Marris College of Hindustani Music.

In 1905 the Badshah Bagh estate comprising about ninety acres was handed to the authorities of the Canning College. Sir John Prescott Hewett, Lieutenant-Governor of the Province, laid the foundation-stone of the new College in 1909, and performed the opening ceremony in 1911. Little remains of the original buildings. The new ones are fine and imposing surrounded by the traditional restful green lawns and tennis courts.

THE BEGUM KOTHI

THE BEGUM KOTHI MUST NOT be confused with the house of the same name within the Residency enclosure. It stands on the left hand side of Hazrat Ganj, coming from Cantonments. Until 1932 the house including a large group of buildings huddled round the central one was used as the General Post Office.

The Begum Kothi was built by King Amjad Ali Shah in 1844 as a palace for his Queen, Malka Ahad Begum. One authority attributes it to Sa'adat Ali Khan about forty years earlier. Possibly Amjad Ali Shah reconstructed his palace upon the site of a former one.

The building was not conspicuous during the Mutiny until March 1858, when two batteries, including the naval guns of H.M.S. *Shannon*, bombarded it continuously for twenty-four hours and made two breaches in the wall near where Abbott Road now runs. The 93rd Highlanders were ordered to storm the Begum Kothi at these two points, supported by the 4th Punjab Rifles and five hundred of Jung Bahadur's Gurkhas. When the bombardment ceased they charged forward, leaping over a ten-foot ditch and a parapet, and took their opponents completely by surprise, so rapid was their advance. The Grenadier Company led by Captain Middleton and Lieutenant Wood, scrambled through the right hand breach, while the Light Company, headed by Captain Clarke and Lieutenant Macpherson, tackled that on the left. They all dashed headlong into the narrow alleys and courts and buildings in which some five thousand of the enemy were said to be ensconced. They followed to the letter their orders to "Keep well together and use the bayonet; give them the Sikandar Bagh over again."

Although the garrison of the Begum Kothi numbered about five thousand, they made no attempt to meet the British face to face in the open. The fighting was severe for large numbers found their retreat cut off by the rush of the attackers past the rooms, archways and passages where they were concealed. Being unable to escape, they fought desperately. From every loophole, door and window, and from every hidden corner in the dark interior came a deadly fire. Many barriers were forced. Small parties headed by officers took possession of one enclosure after another. They pitched bags of gunpowder fixed with slow matches into the crowded rooms and bayoneted the rebels in every nook and corner. For about two hours the blind and bloody fight raged from court to court, from room to room.

So rapid was the progress of the troops through the buildings that the Begum herself narrowly escaped capture About eighty of her female attendants were taken prisoners and proved an embarrassing encumbrance.

Captain Charles William McDonald of the 93rd Highlanders was wounded by a shell splinter in the right arm at the very beginning of the charge, but he refused to heed it until he was again wounded in the throat, this time mortally. His remains are buried near Dilkusha under an inscription erected by his relations: "In memory of his simple virtues as a Christian and his noble conduct as a soldier."

By the evening the attackers were in possession, at the price of many casualties. The foe had suffered even more heavily.

When the attack was announced by signal gun, the famous Major Hodson of the Guides and Hodson's Horse was at the camp at Headquarters. He at once leapt upon his horse and galloped to the spot. There he plunged into the thick of the fight, being mortally wounded as he attempted to climb a staircase.

He was carried to Banks House in great pain, there to die the next morning saying, "I trust I have done my duty." He lies buried in La Martinière park near the College under one of the finest epitaphs that have ever been written : "Here lieth all that could die of William Stephen Raikes Hodson." One of the few that can be compared with it is the inscription on the grave of Sir Henry Lawrence in the Residency cemetery—"Here lies Henry Lawrence, who tried to do his duty."

BIBIAPUR KOTHI

About a mile to the south-east of Dilkusha lies the Bibiapur Kothi, shielded from view by the Government Dairy Farm.

The two-storeyed building is solid and stands on high ground to command a fine view of the country. Originally surrounded by a big park, its origin is shrouded in obscurity, but it was built under the direction of General Claude Martin for Nawab Asaf-ud-Doulah who stayed there from time to time, using it as a hunting box. Its chief use was as a guest house for the incoming British Resident when a change of officials took place. Incidentally it was from here that Sir John Shore (afterwards Lord Teignmouth) had issued the deposition orders of the usurper Wazir Ali, alleged son of Nawab Asaf-ud-Doulah, in 1798 ; at the same time summoning Sa'adat Ali Khan from Benares and welcoming him with an impressive durbar at Bibiapur before taking him in procession to the city where he was proclaimed Nawab.

Years later, in 1856, Colonel Outram received instructions from Lord Dalhousie to proceed to Lucknow from Calcutta to acquaint the King of Oudh with the terms of a treaty.

On nearing Lucknow the newly-appointed Resident was escorted by a detachment of irregular cavalry. The road was lined all the way by crowds anxious to see the man to whom the destinies of their state had been committed. When approaching the Char Bagh, a salute was fired by the Oudh Artillery announcing that the Resident had nearly completed his journey. On these occasions it was the etiquette that the Resident should not enter the city but stay as guest at some garden palace belonging to the King. On his arrival another royal salute from His Majesty's guns proclaimed the presence of the Resident to the public. When he had resided outside the city for the time demanded by etiquette, the reigning King advanced to meet him with all the pomp and ceremony at his command.

An eye-witness of the occasion when Outram arrived as Resident, in December 1856, describes the scene of splendour. Long before sunrise thousands upon thousands crowded the roads and clambered upon the roof of every-building whence they could catch a glimpse of the procession.

A guard of honour consisting of the flank companies of the 19th, 34th and the 2nd Oudh regiments, their colours flying, were drawn up in the park to do honour to Colonel Outram and to salute the heir-apparent.

The troops were officered by Europeans under the command of Major Troup. Accompanying them was the band of the 19th Regiment. "Let the reader imagine a procession of more than three hundred elephants and camels, caparisoned and decorated with all that 'barbaric pomp' could lavish and Asiatic splendour shower down, with all the princes and nobles of the kingdom blazing with jewels, sparkling with gems, gorgeous in apparel, with footmen and horsemen in splendid liveries, swarming on all sides, pennons and banners dancing in the sun's rays, and a perfect forest of gold and silver sticks, spears and other insignia of imperial and royal state."

Slowly and with stately tread the procession approached the newly-appointed official. With equal pomp and gravity the Resident's coach advanced to meet it. As the King and his new adviser met, the guns again thundered forth a royal salute. The Englishman took his place beside the King, whereupon the whole procession retraced its steps to the city. The way was a sea of heads, their owners decked in gala attire. The heir-apparent presented the newcomer with a bag of Rs. 1,200 for distribution amongst the crowds of beggars and vagrants who, as ever, shouted *baksheesh, baksheesh!*

LUCKNOW BRIDGES

UNTIL THE TWENTIETH century there were but two bridges spanning the Gumti at Lucknow, one iron and the other of stone. The latter was begun by the second Nawab, Safdar Jang or Mansur Ali Khan, whose first name is perhaps best known from his tomb at Delhi.

The erection of the bridge dragged slowly on. It was finally completed by the fourth Nawab, Asaf-ud-Doulah, Safdar Jang's grandson. It stood near the existing Hardinge Bridge. Above the delicate tracery of the Mosque of Aurangzeb, abutted upon the more solid outlines of the Machhi Bhawan Fort, high stone walls commanding the coming and going of all who entered and left Lucknow by way of the river.

Early in the present century the bridge was condemned as unsafe and was demolished in 1911 to make way for the Hardinge Bridge which was opened on January 1, 1914, by Lord Hardinge, then Viceroy and Governor-General of India. At the same time he performed the inauguration ceremony of the King George's Hospital. Upon the bridge a tablet states: "This bridge was constructed by the Public Works Department in place of the Nawabi Bridge, which was situated about fifty yards downstream and was built in 1780 by Asaf-ud-Doulah, Nawab-Wazir of Oudh."

Lord Hastings visited Lucknow in 1814 and mentions that the stone bridge over the Gumti, although a handsome structure originally, was in a state of decay. He expressed surprise that the Nawab did not repair it but was told that the Nawab had a firm conviction that repairing the bridge would infallibly cause his death within the year.

Bridges seemed connected with superstition in the minds of the Nawabs, for Bishop Heber who visited Lucknow in 1824 mentions in his observations the broad and rapid stream of the Gumti, where there was a fine old bridge, but one which might in a few minutes be rendered impassable by any force without a regular siege. He goes on to say: "There are two bridges over the Gumty, one a very noble old Gothic edifice of stone of, I believe, eleven arches ; the other a platform laid on boats, and merely connecting the King's park with his palace. Sa'adur Ali has brought over an iron bridge from England and a place was prepared for its erection, but on his death the present sovereign declined to prosecute the work on the ground that it was unlucky, so that in all probability it will lie where it is till the rust reduces it to powder." This was the Iron Bridge which came from England in 1798 and, as has been said, lay in the cases in which it had arrived for over forty years.

The Iron Bridge was conceived by Rennie only twenty years after the first iron bridge had been made in England. It bears a resemblance to the one designed by him at Boston, Lincolnshire, over the River Witham. Rennie's name once more came into prominence during the hard-fought controversy over Waterloo Bridge, also built to his design.

Early in the nineteenth century a steam boat lay on the river, a vessel fitted up like a brig of war, bearing testimony to the King's fondness for mechanical inventions. "He had a skilful English mechanic in his service, and himself knew more of the science and of the different branches of philosophy connected with it, than could be expected in one who understood no language save his own."

General Martin who died in 1800 probably suggested that Sa'adat Ali Khan should purchase the iron bridge. In 1856 Polehampton refers to the English iron bridge as well as a handsome one on brick piers, plastered and coloured yellow.

During Nasr-ud-Din Haider's reign, he directed his engineer, a Mr. Sinclair, to erect the bridge ; he constructed piers for it in front of the Residency, but for some reason the project was once more discontinued. The bridge was finally placed in position between 1842 and 1847 under the direction of Colonel Fraser at a cost of Rs. 180,000 excluding the actual iron work.

Further downstream is the Bruce Bridge, known locally as Monkey Bridge, leading to the University buildings. The house immediately on the left, now occupied by the Vice-Chancellor of the University, was known as the Kabootar Wali Kothi, or Pigeon House, "a poultry yard of beautiful pigeons."

About sixty yards to the east of this bridge blocks of masonry may still be seen on either bank. These formed the approaches to the Bridge of Boats, existent in 1857—over which the mutineers made their escape after the capture by Havelock of the Moti Mahal palaces.

A little further down is the bridge in Sultan Ganj on Outram Road, which, with two railway bridges, makes a total of six all of which cross the river at Lucknow. There are also numerous ferries.

Between 1814 and 1827 King Ghazi-ud-Din Haider decided to build a canal to bring the waters of the Ganges across to the Gumti, thus irrigating parts of Hardoi, Unao and Lucknow. The work was put in the hands of some rascally contractors who carried it out so badly and unscientifically that the project failed, having cost a prodigious sum of money. Four bridges spanned the canal, all of which still exist, one by the Char Bagh, one north of the Sudder Bazaar and two close to Government House.

The old Stone Bridge which had seen so much proud pomp before the gradual decay of Nawabi days, still played a part in 1857, for the gallant Kavanagh who volunteered to make his way out of the Residency to guide Sir Colin Campbell's relieving force into Lucknow, swam across the river and re-entered the city over the Stone Bridge, stealthily keeping under the shadow of the wall. Twice during his perilous journey was he challenged, but he managed to avert suspicion until he finally reached the British camp.

"As he approached, an elderly gentleman with a stern face came out, whom Kavanagh asked for Sir Colin Campbell. 'I am Sir Colin Campbell,' was the sharp reply. Who are you ?"

Kavanagh pulled off his turban and took out a short note of introduction from Sir James Outram.

THE CHUTTER MUNZIL

PROBABLY EVERYBODY knowsthat the United Service Club, otherwise the Greater Chutter Munzil, was once a palace belonging to the Kings of Oudh, but how many realise that formerly there were two storeys below the present three?

Under the existing river terrace was the "ground floor" and

below that again were the *tykhanas,* cooled by the waters of the Gumti which lapped against the outer walls.

Considering their size, surprisingly little is known about the Chutter Munzil Palaces. The name comes from the gilt "chhuttars" or umbrellas at the top of the two main buildings. Their conception is attributed to no less than three Nawabs, Sa'adat Ali Khan, Ghazi-ud-Din, and his son Nasir-ud-Din. Whoever was responsible, present-day experts characterise the building as "a flagrant example of the hybrid style" of Muhammadan architecture allied to debased French or Italian art.

The buildings were intended for the Kings' wives. Originally the palace area extended from the Baillie Gate to some distance beyond the present club entrance, the whole collection being enclosed by a high wall of considerable strength.

The present residential club quarters were known as the Farhat Bakhsh Palace, the property of General Claude Martin who sold it for Rs. 50,000 to King Sa'adat Ali Khan.

Miss Eden who visited Lucknow before the Mutiny went into ecstasies over the Chutter Palaces.

"Such a place," she wrote home to England, "is the only residence I have coveted in India. Don't you remember reading in the Arabian Nights, Zobeide bets her Garden of Delight against the Caleph's Palace of Pictures ? I'm sure this was the Garden of Delight.

"There are four small places in it fitted up in the Eastern way with velvet, gold and marble, with arabesque ceilings, orange trees and roses in all directions and with numerous wild paroquets of bright colours flitting about. And in one place there was an immense *hammam* or Turkish bath of white marble, the arches intersecting each other in all directions and the marble inlaid with cornelian and bloodstone, and in every corner of the palace there were little fountains ; even during the hot winds, they say, it is cool from the quantity of water in the fountains playing ; and in the verandah there were fifty trays of fruits and flowers laid out for us."

Tradition hints at a large tank lying between the Greater and Lesser Chutter, although there is no evidence to prove either that or the supposition that a subterranean passage leads from the Greater Chutter under the river to the far bank of the Gumti.

Other buildings embraced in the term Chutter Munzil are the Darshan-Bilas (Pleasure to the Sight) and the Gulistan-i-Eram (Heavenly Garden), now the Public Works Department offices. Either in the Gulistan-i-Eram or in the Farhat Bakhsh occurred the death of Nasir-ud-Din Haider, the second King of Oudh.

On the night of July 7, 1837 King Nasir-ud-Din accepted from a woman a glass of sherbet, which is said to have contained powdered glass. He died there and then.

For nearly twenty years after that the Chutter buildings again echoed to the soft laughter of women of the royal harem, until the first mutterings of the Mutiny froze the smile upon their lips. By then the out-buildings of the Palace extended almost to the Monkey Bridge, and a perfect web of narrow passages and courtyards had sprung up on the space now presided over by the statue of Her Majesty Queen Victoria.

The Chutter Munzil palaces were important strongholds of the rebels. Their capture had to be effected by the relieving force on their difficult path to the Residency. Late in September 1857, Havelock's column moved towards the Residency to receive a sharp check at the Char Bagh bridge which lay over a canal now forgotten. The resistance was soon overcome, however, with the aid of Maude's battery and a charge by the Fusiliers.

Fighting every foot of the way, the relief column halted beneath the comparative shelter of the Chutter Munzil. Next day they gained the Residency. On November 16, the beleaguered garrison knew that the second relieving force under Sir Colin Campbell was advancing by way of the Sikandar Bagh.

The besieged troops were drawn up in the courtyard of the Chutter Munzil which was reoccupied by the rebels. When the advance sounded at half past three that afternoon, General Havelock says in his report that it was "impossible to describe the enthusiasm with which this signal was received by the troops. Pent up in inaction for upwards of six weeks and subjected to constant attacks, they felt that the hour of retribution and glorious exertion had returned. Their cheers echoed through the courts of the palace, responsive to the bugle sound, and on they rushed to assured victory. The enemy could nowhere withstand them. In a few minutes the whole of the buildings were in our possession." On November 19 when Sir Colin Campbell decided finally to evacuate the Residency, the way to freedom lay through the Chutter Palace area ; from there to the Moti Mahal the route was still subject to musketry fire.

An old legend whispers of an unseen servant who carries a lantern from room to room of the upper storey ; rooms which in the broad light of day are found to be non-existent.

LUCKNOW SHRINES

TWO SHRINES LIE TO THE south-west of the Chauk, a point of pilgrimage for many pious Muhammadans at Moharram time.

The more celebrated of the two was erected to Abbas, an uncle of Ali, who was cousin and son-in-law to the Prophet and who was killed in the battle of Kerbala.

The word *dargah* means sacred threshold or door-place ; hazrat means saint. The shrine of saint Abbas was erected to house the metal crest which crowned the banner of Abbas, "conveyed thither long ago by a poor pilgrim from the west." Hence the pilgrimage when the banners make obeisance on the fifth day of Moharram. During the Moharram banners are carried in procession to the shrine, where their bearers touch with them the sacred relic, before passing through the rear gateway.

About a hundred years ago the Dargah was a fine building some five miles from the King's Palace. Upon a centre platform garnished with bunting and gay flags the sacred crest was fixed upon a pole. On the morning of the fifth day of Moharram crowds visited the shrine, each party bearing its own banner. Naturally enough no one was allowed to eclipse the cortège of the King in magnificence. An advance guard of half-a-dozen gorgeously caparisoned elephants carried the bearers of the banners accompanied by a military guard. Following them came a symbolical chief mourner carrying a black pole upon which hung a bow and two reversed swords.

Behind him came the King with his male relatives. Next was led a charger representative of the one Hosein was riding when he was killed. A grey Arab, on its reddened legs and sides arrows appeared to be buried to indicate the sufferings of horse and rider. A turban in the Arabian style and a bow and quiver of arrows were affixed to the saddle which rested upon a beautifully embroidered saddle-cloth. The trappings were all of solid gold. Attendants, gorgeously dressed, accompanied the horse with fly-whisks made of the yak's tail. Sometimes fifty thousand banners passed through the shrine on this annual date, forming a continual stream from early dawn until dusk.

Occasionally the royal Begums accompanied by all the pomp and circumstance at their command made formal pilgrimage to the shrine. In the van marched the King's bodyguard, resplendent in blue and silver and accompanied by band and colours. They were followed by two battalions of infantry in crimson and a company of spearmen in white, silver spear-heads flashing in the sun. More men in white carrying royal pennants preceded the litter of the Queen which was supported by twenty bearers changed every quarter of a mile. They wore tightly-fitting garments under a loose scarlet coat lavishly adorned with gold embroidery and a scarlet turban, into which was pinned the gold-fish badge of Oudh. The Queen had to be surrounded by women bearers when she embarked or alighted. They marched near the royal litter, followed by the gold and silver sticks, the chief eunuch upon an elephant, the ladies of the court in a heterogeneous collection of vehicles, and finally an entourage of court soldiers, spearmen, story-tellers, hair-dressers, tailors, learned men versed in the Koran, and a hundred others.

Near the Dargah of Hazrat Abbas is the Talkatora Karbala, the rendezvous for the Moharram processions from the city for the final disposal of the tazias. It was built about 1800 by Mir Khuda Baksh Khan, a Naib of Sa'adat Ali Khan, and represents the tomb of Hosein.

DILKUSHA PALACE

The Palace of Dilkusha —"Heart's Delight"—was built by Nawab Sa'adat Ali Khan (1798-1814).

It was erected as a hunting box in the centre of a large park stocked with all manner of game that disported among the great trees. Near by lay a large shallow lake upon which the Nawabs, especially Nasir-ud-Din Haider, would conduct bird shoots. At first shooting was the primary object, with comfort a bad second. As generation succeeded generation, however, the ratios were reversed. Everything was sacrificed to comfort and the birds were so tamed for weeks beforehand that a shoot amounted almost to wholesale slaughter.

In 1814 Lord Hastings, the Governor-General, visited Lucknow and shot in the Dilkusha park but sport was moderate. At that time it had a circumference of about three miles. It was thickly wooded with a dense tropical undergrowth.

In the troubles of 1857 Havelock spent some time discussing routes by which to approach the Residency, one of which was by way of Dilkusha, La Martinière, and the Sikandar Bagh, but ultimately he decided to take a more direct route. On November 14, Sir Colin Campbell, with the second relief force, advanced from the Alam Bagh by way of Dilkusha. The rebels had not expected him to go by this route and were taken by surprise. However, they put up a stiff resistance. After a sharp interchange of hostilities the British force made a breach in the park wall and poured in, driving the enemy pell-mell before them. Two batteries were brought up and placed in position upon a commanding slope to the north-west of Dilkusha Palace and supported the infantry advance.

On November 16, the force pressed hard on their adversary's heels, leaving the Eighth Foot to garrison Dilkusha.

When the relief of the Residency was at last accomplished the main body of the survivors evacuated the position by way of the Sikandar Bagh, and thence to Dilkusha whither the troops, last to leave the historic site, marched by a more direct route through the city.

On November 20, General Havelock fell ill and was taken to Dilkusha. There Sir Colin Campbell visited him on the evening of the 23rd, and wrote later: "I had a most affecting interview with him. His tenderness was that of a brother. He told me he was dying and spoke from the fulness of his honest heart of the feelings which he bore towards me, and of the satisfaction with which he looked back to our past intercourse and service together, which had never been on a single occasion marred by a disagreement of any kind, nor embittered by an angry word. How truly I mourned his loss is known to God and my own heart." The next morning the great soldier breathed his last. Havelock died fearlessly, saying only a few minutes before the end, "I have, for forty years, so ruled my life that when death came I might face it without fear." He was buried in a soldier's modest grave at the Alam Bagh the next day.

Several others lie buried beneath the shadow of the crumbling walls. Among them are Lieutenant Paul of the 4th Punjab Rifles, who was killed at the Sikandar Bagh, Captain Macdonald of the 93rd Highlanders who, "although he had been a Captain for some years, was still almost a boy", and Lieutenant Charles Dashwood, affectionately known to the whole garrison as Charlie Dashwood. He had been through the entire siege and had both his legs shot off while sketching in the gardens of the Residency. An operation was performed, but his health was too weak to stand it, and he died from exhaustion when freedom was within sight.

When the troubled land was once more peaceful, Dilkusha

was restored and became the residenee of the General Commanding the Oudh Division, until it was declared to be unsafe. It was partially demolished and lies almost derelict now. From the top of the tower there is a fine panorama of Lucknow and its surroundings, peaceful and prosperous at last.

THE GREAT IMAMBARA

THE GREAT IMAMBARA IS a stately building pronounced to be one of the most imposing in the world. It lies within the area known as the Machhi Bhawan Fort long ago demolished. It was built by Nawab Asaf-ud-Doulah in the year 1784 at a cost of a crore of rupees (about one million pounds). Only a few years before his father, Shuja-ud-Doulah, had transferred his royal residence from Fyzabad to Lucknow, so that there was scope in plenty for the erection of magnificent buildings.

The Great Imambara was constructed as a famine relief measure for the stricken city populace. The Nawab caused architects throughout India to compete for the plans, stating that the building was to be unique in structure and that it was to surpass every known building in grandeur. The designs of Kifayat-ullah, a well-known architect, were accepted and the work was commenced. It is said that to afford relief to some of the noble families who, without detriment to their social position, could not be seen engaged in such menial labour, payment was made at night in the dark, without inquiry concerning the identity of the recipient.

With the exception of the galleries in the interior no wood is used in the construction. The central apartment is said to be the largest vaulted hall in the world. The inside measurements are a hundred and sixty-three feet long by fifty-three feet broad by forty-nine and a half feet high, and the walls vary from ten to sixteen feet in thickness and contain passages long since closed.

It is believed that there are large underground chambers, but the passages leading to them have been blocked up since the last century. From the central chamber a staircase leads to a series of rooms designed as a maze. Above these again is a flat roof.

The Imambara is approached by an imposing square gateway surmounted by an octagonal pavilion, and the entire facade is pierced by a myriad arched window openings. Beyond the three doorways in the base lies a garden quadrangle. At the end steps lead up to a portal similar to the first. Three fine wrought-iron doors lead to a second garden terrace on the left of which is a line of cloisters concealing a well, very old and very deep, built in grandiose style, with a balcony above and steps leading to the water's edge. In the centre of the main chamber is the tomb of Asaf-ud-Doulah. Near him lie the remains of the architect.

"Imambara" is a general term for a building in which the festival of the Moharram is celebrated, sometimes used, as in this case, for a mausoleum. In contrast to a "masjid" which is unornamented in order that the attention of the worshippers shall not be distracted from their prayers an "Imambara" is a building dedicated to the memory of the three Imams, Ali and Hassan and Hussain, his sons, and lavishly decorated in their honour. Colonel Newell says of the Great Imambara that its usual daily routine is that of any well-ordered museum or historical show-place. Once a year, however, it awakens from this official lethargy. All its myriad crystal chandeliers burst into sudden flame, and the tomb and tazias assume still further splendours in honour of the Moharram.

Bishop Heber, who visited Lucknow in 1824 when the Great Imambara was about forty years old, describes it thus:—"This tabernacle of chandeliers was hung with immense lustres of silver and gold, prismatic crystals, and coloured glass, and any that were too heavy to be hung rose in radiant piles from the floor. In the midst of them were temples of silver filigree, eight or ten feet high and studded with precious stones. There were ancient banners of the Nawabs of Oudh, with sentences from the Koran embroidered on cloth of gold; gigantic bands of silver covered with talismanic words; sacred shields studded with the name of God; swords of

Khorasan steel, lances, and halberds ; the turbans of renowned commanders ; and several pulpits of peculiar sanctity..."

In 1856 the Rev. Henry Polehampton described the "Imaum Barrah" as "a large quadrangle, about the same size as 'Tom Quad' at Christ Church, surrounded by very beautiful buildings. At the farther end is the King's tomb. It is contained in a large hall full of all sorts of curiosities. There are many immense chandeliers from England, remarkable only for size ; and a wooden horse, from a saddler's shop in Calcutta, is highly prized. With all this there are some beautiful shrines of silver. The King's tomb is one. It is about eight feet long and four broad, all silver, as also is his mother's. In the court are tanks of water, something like those at the Crystal Palace ; and by the side are creepers trained, and the prettiest is a little red flower.... At the Imaum Barrah end of the city the streets are very wide and, thanks to the English, perfectly clean and hard. The steward of the palace which is richly endowed took daguerreotypes, the early form of photographs, and was a very gentlemanly man, a Mahommedan, and most liberal. He won't take anything for his likenesses. He gives you freely as many as you want, and takes no end of trouble."

During the reign of Nasir-ud-Din Haider two square courts extended in front of the building of the Imambara, decorated with tessellated pavements. The inner was raised several feet above the outer.

The Durgah, five miles from the King's palace, contained the metal crest of the banner of Husain, and on the morning of the fifth day of Moharram people of all ranks and classes went in procession to visit it. The procession from the Royal Imambara was most magnificent, preceded by six or eight gorgeously caparisoned elephants, and escorted by a military guard. Following them came a man bearing a black pole upon which two swords hung from a reversed bow. Then came the King, the male members of his family, and his Moulvis. Behind them was led a white Arab horse wearing a richly embroidered saddle cloth and trappings of solid gold, with reddened flanks to imitate arrow wounds, and finally many servants and followers.

To the north-east of the main building a mosque stands on a raised platform, flanked by minarets over a hundred and fifty feet high, each with a staircase leading to the top. This is the only mosque in Lucknow where the Friday prayers for the Shia sect are said.

The Imambara Trust is managed by a committee and various ceremonies take place during the year. At each of these, cooked food or sweets are distributed among the audience, and on the ninth day of the Moharram illuminations continue throughout the night. The Trust sends about eighty pilgrims every year to Kerbala, each of whom is given a hundred and fifty rupees. During the month of Ramzan cooked food is distributed daily to over six hundred people. Families in reduced circumstances are given allowances and lodging in the Rais Munzil, and the Trust also maintains the gardens.

THE HAYAT BAKHSH KOTHI

GOVERNMENT HOUSE stands on the site of the original Hayat Bakhsh Kothi, built during the reign of Nawab Sa'adat Ali Khan between 1793 and 1814, and originally used by General Claud Martin as a powder magazine.

When Sa'adat Ali Khan came to the throne he found that his predecessor and half-brother, Asaf-ud-Doulah, had left many debts behind him. At first he made no attempt to grapple with them but continued in the same vein of extravagance until he found himself in difficulties. After some deliberation, he came to a compromise with the East India Company which thus, in 1801, acquired official status in Oudh.

Some years later, about 1856, the Hayat Bakhsh Kothi became the residence of the Commissioner of Lucknow, and was known as Banks' House. The first Commissioner was a Major Banks, whose name still persists in Major Banks Road. There is in existence to-day an enlargement of a daguerreotype taken of Banks' House at that period. It shows a double-storeyed building with thatched verandah roofs.

It had a pillared porch and stood upon a plinth, but beyond that it had no marked resemblance to the handsome spaciously-verandahed residence of the Governors of the United Provinces. The daguerreotype shows underground rooms untraceable to-day. Probably much of the original house was pulled down in 1907 when the ball-room and a wing of guest suites were added.

Major John Sherbrooke Banks was a son of Surgeon S. Banks, of His Majesty's Service. He joined the Indian Army in 1829 and went to the 33rd Regiment of Native Infantry. Later he volunteered for civil duties, and went on a tour with Lord Dalhousie to Burma. In 1857 he was Commissioner of Lucknow. When Sir Henry Lawrence was mortally wounded in the Residency and knew that he was dying, he appointed Colonel Inglis to command the troops and Major Banks as Chief Commissioner.

The latter, however, did not long survive to hold that arduous post, for the garrison had scarcely recovered from the shock of the loss of its revered and beloved general, when it mourned the death of Major Banks who took a bullet through his head while examining a critical out-post on July 21. He died without a sound and lies buried in the Residency cemetery.

During the second relief, Sir Colin Campbell instructed Brigadier Russell to clear up several ruined bungalows in the area between the present Wingfield Park and Hazratganj. This they did, and a specially detailed party of the 2nd Punjab Infantry occupied Banks House with no resistance.

After the withdrawal of the British from every part of Lucknow at the end of 1857, the stronger points of vantage were naturally re-occupied by the rebels. In 1858 the cleaning up process had to be gone through again. On March 6, Sir James Outram crossed the Gumti with a large force, while two batteries of guns opened fire against the Martinière and the canal works respectively.

Four days later the second of these two batteries, reinforced by another, bombarded Banks' House. At noon it was stormed and taken without much difficulty by part of the 2nd Infantry division under Sir Edward Lugard, and made into a strong military base.

On March 11, that famous and gallant soldier, William Stephen Raikes Hodson, of Hodson's Horse, fell mortally wounded in the assault on the Begum Kothi. He was carried in great pain to Banks' House, where he died in one of the lower rooms early the next morning saying: "I trust I have done my duty." The khaki-clad figure of Major Hodson is supposed still to visit the house and to walk through the rooms.

HAZRATGANJ

"AT LAST WE SUDDENLY ENTERED A very handsome street indeed, wider than the High Street at Oxford, but having some distant resemblance to it in the colour of its buildings and the general form and Gothic style of thegreater part of them." Such was Lucknow's main street in 1824.

Twenty years or so later the traffic had grown out of all

proportion to the size of the streets, especially as elephants were used. Nothing could be more ludicrous than the incongruity between the huge animals and the narrow, confined streets in which they once had to travel. One blocked up the entire road. In the lower and filthier parts of the town horses were seldom seen, elephants and camels being the common carriers.

Men of rank were accompanied by armed retainers in proportion to station and wealth. It was by no means unusual for fights to occur between these bands in the narrow streets.

The term *Hazrat* is equivalent to Saint. Noah and Abraham and Christ are spoken of by Mussalmans as Hazrat Noah, Hazrat Ibrahim and Hazrat Isa (Jesus). Fashions change in streets as in everything else, and what was once termed a street of noble width had in 1856 become a narrow road, with tall houses rising from either side. A year later these same houses were strongly fortified.

In the angle made by Hazratganj and Outram Road, stands Lawrence Terrace, now the premises of the Lucknow (Residency) Club. The buildings are long and low, built by Nawab Sa'adat Ali Khan at the beginning of the nineteenth century for the Royal Chaupar stables. In 1856 they were turned into barracks and occupied by the men of the 32nd Regiment whose officers used the Khurshaed Munzil as their Mess House and had their quarters between the Allahabad Bank and Christ Church. The barracks were two immense squares with low buildings all round, housing the men who had been reorganised into ten companies of a hundred each.

A little further along the Ganj a small site is now occupied by a branch of a well-known shoe manufacturer. On March 10, 1858, a gun emplacement was hastily constructed on that spot. From it, mortars and the naval guns of H. M. S. *Shannon* were trained for twenty-four hours upon the Begum Kothi on the opposite side of the road. Another battery stood at the corner of Hazratganj opposite the Allahabad Bank, about a hundred and fifty yards from the Church, and bombarded the rear of the Begum Kothi. The Dar-ul-Shafa is popularly supposed to have been originally a hospital, but no records remain to confirm this. Nawab Sa'adat Ali Khan stayed there to undergo treatment for a serious carbuncle at the hands of Dr. Law and Mirza Janzi, a native physician. They managed to cure him. Beyond that no details are available.

Returning to Hazratganj, the next building, proceeding towards the Chutter Munzil, on the left hand side, is the Kothi Sultan Inayat, which was the part of the Begum Kothi, later used as the General Post Office. Further along past the shops, where Hazratganj is again called the Mall, on the right hand side of the road, stands the square and solid Kankar Wali Kothi. This was built by King Ghazi-ud-Din Haider between 1814 and 1827, but otherwise has little historical interest. Farther along on the opposite side of the road stands the Nur Bakhsh Kothi, or Light-Giving House, now the residence of Deputy Commissioners of Lucknow. Some say that it was built by Nawab Sa'adat Ali Khan as a *Maktab* for his grandson, Rafi-ush-Shan. Other authorities state that it was built by Agha Mir, Prime Minister to King Ghazi-ud-Din Haider. When Nasir-ud-Din Haider succeeded Ghazi-ud-

Din in 1827, Agha Mir somehow fell out with his new master and had to leave Lucknow, so that his property including several handsome buildings was confiscated by the King. In 1837 Muhammad Ali Shah came to the throne and presented the Nur Bakhsh to his son Mirza Rafi-ush-Shan who lived there until 1857.

When Sir Henry Havelock advanced to the first relief of the Residency he stood upon the top of the Nur Baksh overlooking the enemy's entrenchments and made his plan.

Within the house stands a tomb popularly reputed to be haunted.

THE HUSAINABAD IMAMBARA

"THE PALACE OF LIGHTS."

THE HUSAINABAD Imambara : such was the name given by King Muhammad Ali Shah to the only building he completed during his short reign of five years. He succeeded the most famous, or perhaps the most notorious, of the rulers of Oudh, Nasir-ud-Din Haider, in spite of the efforts of the Queen Begum to place her adopted grandson,

Moona Jan, on the throne.

Muhammad Ali Shah was already old and feeble at the time of his accession, and later he became completely bed-ridden. Even then he took an interest in his city and concentrated his efforts upon Husainabad. Sir Henry Lawrence, three years after the death of Muhammad Ali Shah, wrote that Lucknow "consisted of an old and a new city adjoining each other. The former was filthy, ill-drained and ill-ventilated." The new city consisted of broad airy streets, giving on to the Royal Palaces and gardens, the principal mosque, the Residency, and the houses of the various English officers connected with the court. European architecture mingled strangely with oriental buildings. Travellers compared it to Moscow and Constantinople. Guilded domes surmounted by the crescent, tall slender pillars, lofty colonnades, houses that might have been transplated from Regent Street, iron railings and balustrades, gardens, fountains and cypress trees, elephants, camels and horses, gilded litters and English barouches, all formed a pleasing kaleidoscope.

Following the custom of his forbears, Muhammad Ali Shah built the Husainabad Imambara as his tomb. Modern taste condemns it as a tawdry building with marked degeneration of intellectual taste. Tawdry it is, although it seems to have struck differently eyes that beheld it in all its pristine freshness. A Russian prince, Alexis Soltykoff, visited Lucknow in 1841 and wrote that at the end of a large and busy street was a magnificent Moorish gate-way, beyond which rose "gracefully proportioned minarets with gilded cupolas, like those of the Kremlin of Moscow. These together with the avenue crowded with fantastic people produced a superb effect. The gateway led to the walled enclosure which the old King had chosen for his last resting-place. I went inside and was astounded to find that the enclosure contained a collection of all that was charming and amusing: several Moorish edifices of marvellous design, fountains, aviaries in which were most extraordinary and beautiful birds. Some of the buildings were still under construction. They are intended to be places of resort for the people on fête days. The King's mother rests in the largest building under a miniature silver-gilt mosque. This building is composed of four or five vaulted chambers separated by pillars and arcades." At that time it was filled with innumerable crystal chandeliers, glass and silver, and painted wooden horses and tigers. Some fifteen months later, von Orlich visited Lucknow when the body of Muhammad Ali Shah was lying in a silver sarcophagus in the building designed for its reception.

A small bazaar, known as the Gelo Khana or "Decorated Place", lies inside the imposing entrance of the Imambara and is the home of *chikan* and *bidri* workers and of those who make the small clay figures peculiar to Lucknow. Opposite the entrance is a similar structure, the Naubat Khana, where seven musicians play three times a day in honour of the dead.

The royal fish coat of arms adorns the gateway which is guarded by curious female figures for whose lower limbs are substituted those of a horse. Inside is a large courtyard where a rectangular raised tank occupies much of the centre spanned by a small bridge. A decorative barge floats on the water. Graceful cypress trees adorn the edges. Two gilt statues are chained from the ground to the top of the gateway, while on each side of the courtyard is a small imitation of the Taj Mahal at Agra. In one is buried Muhammad Ali Shah's daughter, Zenab Asuja, and in the other are relics of her husband who died too far from Lucknow to allow of his remains being brought to the resting place intended for them.

At the far end, past a small mosque reserved for descendants of the royal family, a wide flight of steps leads to the main shrine where Muhammad Ali Shah and his mother lie buried. Heavy silver railings surround each tomb and nearby stand the King's silver throne, several costly tazias, and two copies of the Koran said to be of a great age and to have been brought originally from Mecca.

Muhammad Ali Shah, whose full title was His Majesty Abdul-fateh Muin-uddin Sultan-uz-zaman Nausherwani-Adil Muhammad Ali Shah, third King of Oudh, originally endowed this Imambara in 1839 with an income of twelve lakhs of rupees invested in the East Indian Company's four per cent. loan. He added securities worth twenty-four lakhs to assist members of the Shia sect to proceed to Kerbala on pilgrimage, to relieve the sufferings of the poor and needy, and for the performance of divers religious ceremonies. In 1878 the Government of India passed an act to provide for the better management of the endowment. The Imambara stands to-day as a monument to the one King who tried to arrest the rapid decay of morals and physique which ultimately caused the downfall of the Kingdom.

THE JAMA MASJID

Leaving the great Imambara on the left and driving a few yards through the Rumi Darwaza, the traveller may get his first view of the Jama Masjid, standing in commanding isolation overlooking the city. The story of Oudh is one of gathering speed on the downward path, to which each King of Oudh gave impetus ; Muhammad Ali Shah alone tried to arrest the descent. But when he succeeded to the throne of Oudh in 1837 he was already feeble in health, and during his short reign he became almost completely bed-ridden. He concentrated upon Husainabad, and planned to beautify that quarter of the city. It is said that the Sat Khanda, of which only four of the intended seven storeys were completed at his death in 1842, was designed that he might lie on the roof storey and survey the work going on around him.

He inaugurated the Jama Masjid intending it to eclipse every other mosque in Lucknow, even the Great Imambara, but at his death it was still unfinished. Begum Malka Jahan, one of the begums of the royal family, saw to its completion a short time later. One authority says that Muhammad Ali Shah gave to one of his wives, Malka Jahan, the sum of ten lakhs to spend as she willed, and with part of this money she built the Jama Masjid.

"Masjid" is an Arabic word meaning "House of Prayer". The Jama Masjid follows the usual form of a square building surmounted by three domes, and having a tall slender minaret at either front corner, from which the Muezzin calls to the faithful at the appointed hour: "God is great: Come to Prayer: Come to salvation."

The Jama Masjid has beauty of proportion apparent from every angle. It has a lofty doorway ornamented in stucco, painted an unusual cool green with touches of white and brick red. The interior is plain so that nothing shall distract the attention of the worshippers. Only in the wall facing the entrance is a niche showing the direction of Mecca to which worshippers must turn their faces. This mosque is used for the weekly Friday prayers of the Shias.

To one side lie the ruins of what must once have been a large brick building. It has been impossible to gather information about its origin. It may have been a Muhammadan school but now makes a delightful frame for one side of the mosque, its deep weathered red mingling with the peculiarly olive green foliage of the trees which have pushed their way through the masonry. All around are evidences of the departed Nawabi days, other mosques and palaces crumbling to dust, still impressive by their very size and by the hint of past glories suggested by great doorways and balustrades silhouetted against the sky.

On rising ground to the right front of the Jama Masjid lies a Mohammadan graveyard, hiding from view a small but celebrated house, the Pili Kothi or Yellow House. Its origin is shrouded in oblivion but it is believed to have been the residence of the King's physician.

On September 23, 1857 the force coming to the help of the garrison from Cawnpore fought a fierce action to possess the Alam Bagh. In the heat of success, Outram himself led a mounted pursuit of the enemy which took them nearly as far as the Yellow House, a distance of four or five miles. The British troops withdrew to the Alam Bagh and spent the next day refitting and repairing and at 8 a. m. on the 25th they started off again. Directly they came within range of the men concealed in every house along the way, they were subjected to a fierce musketry fire. The Yellow House concealed two guns which wreaked havoc among the British troops, the more so because the rear of the column was not ready to start. The order was passed up to halt. At last the

"Advance" sounded, and the enemy was forced to fall back upon the Yellow House while the British force pushed past it, leaving it on the right flank.

Later in the day the guns, cunningly placed in the Yellow House, were swung round to operate effectively upon the rear of their enemy until, by order of General Havelock, the 90th stormed the house in face of a heavy fire and captured the guns. They were actually carried off by Major Olpherts who won the V.C. for this gallant action.

The Yellow House to-day presents a modest front—or rather side—to the road. It is two-storeyed with a flat roof. Deep yellow wash still persists, while the balustrade around the roof is ornamented with tiny green pillars half buried in the wall. Inside, a circular staircase at one corner leads to little rooms washed in bright colours and with raised contrasting friezes. The designs and the sham venetian blinds show the influence of Western fashions. Each end of the house is built to form a deep bay window. An entrance porch supported by wooden pillars sagging badly gives on to a tiny wilderness of garden. Below a wing built at right angles to the house are immense underground rooms. The present owner bought it some years ago meaning to repair it and to live in it, but he found that the ravages of war and time had sunk too deep, so he built himself a little white villa with a charming garden alongside.

JOHN COLLINS

NOT TEN MINUTES' DRIVE FROM THE Chutter Munzil Palaces, in a mohulla called Lat Kalan-ki-Lat. stands a high-walled enclosure surrounded by narrow bazaar streets. The gate is high and riveted and made of iron bars. Inside, in a disused European cemetery, are some forty or fifty pretentious monuments, the sepulchral leaden inscriptions on them long since gone. Records tell us that among others Colonel Wilcox, one time Astronomer Royal, lies there. The most ambitious memorial of all bears an inscription which remains because it happens to be carved in the stone itself:—

In Memory
of
Colonel John Collins
Resident at the Court of Lucknow
1806-7
Died 18*th June*, 1807

The monument stands almost in front of the gate not ten yards away. From it is derived the name of the mohulla, Lat Kalan-ki-Lat, "the tomb of Lord Collins."

John Collins joined the East India Company's Bengal Infantry in 1770, rising to the rank of Major after twenty-four years' service. A year later he became Resident at the Court of Daulat Rao Sindhia who thought well of him but nevertheless persisted in intriguing against the British Raj. After the Treaty of Bassein, Major Collins discovered and reported that Daulat Rao was involved in various plots. Declaration of war against Sindhia followed.

In 1799, Wazir Ali who had been deposed from the throne of Oudh after a reign of three months, resided in the garden of one Madho Das in Benares. The British knew that Wazir Ali was plotting against them. They ordered him to go to Calcutta. This infuriated him. On January 14, he visited Mr. Cherry, Agent to the Governor-General in Benares, and basely stabbed him.

At the same time Mr. Evans, a secretary, was killed near by, according to plan, and Captain Canway was cut down by Wazir Ali's retinue as he rode up the drive of Mr. Cherry's house. The insurgents then made for the house of Mr. Davis, Judge and Magistrate, killing Mr. Graham on the way. Mr. Davis lived at what is now Nandesar House, the guest house of the Maharajah. Sensing their intent, Mr Davis snatched up a hog-spear and defended himself at the head of a narrow winding staircase which led to the roof. This same staircase now leads to a sleeping apartment. He kept his enemies at bay until General Erksine arrived with a small body of troops. But Wazir Ali made good his escape. A reward of Rs. 20,000 was offered for his head and he took refuge with the Raja of Jaipur. The Raja proved a false friend betraying him to the British. Colonel Collins was sent to Jaipur to receive his surrender. A few years later "King Collins", so named for a "cold, imperious and over-bearing manner", became Resident at the Court of Oudh and died a few months after he had taken office.

THE KAISER BAGH PALACES

WAJID ALI SHAH, the last King of Oudh, who came to the throne in 1847, started to build the Kaiser Bagh Palaces the year after his accession, intending to make them the eighth wonder of the world. The buildings were completed in 1850. Rumour had it that their cost exceeded eighty lakhs and that the area they covered was greater than that of the

Tuileries and the Louvre put together. So eager was the King for quantity that, as with most of his inspirations, quality was forgotten. All that now remains of his enormous conception are buildings on three sides of a quadrangle.

Somewhere near the tennis courts of the Oudh Gymkhana Club stood the Jilankhana, a triumphal gateway whence royal processions wound their way through dense crowds of applauding citizens. Another gateway led to the Chini Bagh ornamented with Chinese vases and decorations, the Lakhi Gate which as its name implies cost a lakh of rupees, the Kilo Khana, the Hazrat Bagh, the Chandiwala Baradari with its floor of polished silver, and many others now only names instead of grandiose buildings.

Wajid Ali Shah was fond of singing and dancing. He even dressed in female garments himself and danced before the ladies of the harem. Every year he acted in a play—always the same one.

One of his wives was chosen to represent Ghyzalah, and as she was beautiful, the honour of representing her was eagerly sought in the harem; others were dressed as peris with silver wings. Another represented Rajah Indra, the king of fairies of Hindu mythology. Others were dressed up as evil genii and their attendants with black ornaments, black wings and black faces. None wished to act these last parts, but at the expression of the King's wishes none could refuse. The play was enacted in the silver baradari of the Kaiser Bagh palace in Lucknow, which was divided for the purpose into three compartments. One of these was fitted up as Rajah Indra's court, the pillars covered with silver and rich ornaments attached to the ceiling and walls. At night it was a blaze of light with chandeliers and mirrors. In the centre stood Indra's throne, and there the lady representing him sat in state clothes in rich apparel and attended by crowds of peris.

Without, fountains of scented water played. The seats of the garden were gilded or silvered over to shine amid the flowers and fountains lit up during the day by the sun's rays and at night by a myriad lamps. For ten days and nights this pageant continued. Another room was fitted up as a royal bedroom. A golden bedstead, a rich counterpane, a magnificent carpet, and golden furniture framed the beautiful Ghyzalah, her delicate limbs in gauze or muslin edged with golden tissue, her black hair shining with gems. On the tenth day, the King danced for the entertainment of the multitude and insisted upon the queen and Khas Mehal and other leading ladies of the court giving him presents of money.

The yellow buildings round the quadrangle are now the property of the Taluqdars of Oudh as town houses. Gateways on either side, bearing a resemblance to the crown surmounting La Martinière College, are ornamented with the royal fish badge. Massive doors studded with curious iron plaques swing on rusted hinges.

It is possible to walk for some distance along the flat roofs. The rooms within are long and not very lofty, with deep verandahs giving on to the central court.

Many of the King's most precious treasures (not to mention his harem numbering nearly four hundred, each of whom occupied a suite of rooms and had her own attendants) were housed in the Kaiser Bagh, and the mutineers made it one of their most formidable strongholds in 1857.

In the fighting at the Moti Mahal during the first relief the British troops were much harassed by fire from the Kaiser Bagh. The 78th Highlanders fought their way along the Hazratganj and suddenly found themselves on the flank of the enemy battery which was causing most of the trouble. The Highlanders made a rush to spike the guns before pressing on and joining the main column.

During the second relief musketry fire from the Kaiser Bagh again swept the ranks of the relieving troops. From November 20 to 22 the full force of British guns was turned on it. This was after the Residency had been evacuated by the women and children. By the 22nd three wide breaches had been made in the walls and the entire enemy resources were mustered at these points, for an assault was expected. Attention thus diverted from the Residency, shortly before mid-night the gallant little personnel of the Residency collected at the Bailey Guard gateway and silently filed out.

Early in March 1858 the enemy again fortified the Kaiser Bagh with three lines of entrenchments including the canal. On March 13, the Sikhs attached to the British force penetrated into an outlying court of the Kaiser Bagh. From the roofs of the houses they fired upon the men below, to drive them from the guns. This so weakened the defences that Napier and Franks held a rapid consultation and decided to concentrate their entire strength upon the Kaiser Bagh. During this attack Captain L. S. Da Costa, 56th Native Infantry, was killed. He lies buried near Major Hodson in La Martinière Park. Franks' column attacked from the enclosure of Sa'adat Ali Khan's tomb and joined the main body of soldiers, sailors, Gurkhas and Sikhs in the courts of the palace. The bulk of the attack was broken but armed men found refuge in the buildings, and every palace became a fortress. From the green Venetian blinds closing the apertures which pierce the walls in double rows, a stream of bullets poured into the square, so that the marble pavement was stained with the blood of Sikh and Briton.

"Building after building was taken and bloodthirst revenge and greed for gold glutted the avarice of the Sikh and the British soldier. Rough hands tore away the silks, velvets, brocades, laces and gems accumulated by the lights of the Harem ; wrought silver plates were torn from the throne of some favourite mistress or queen ; the monuments of western and eastern art were broken to pieces, and fragments of rare China and of crystal vessels strewed the floors. When night put an end to the pillage, the palace of the Kaiser had become a ruined charnel-house."

THE KHURSHAED MUNZIL

KHURSHAED MUNZIL means " House of the Sun." It was named by Nawab Sa'adat Ali Khan after one of his favourite wives, Khurshaed Zadi, for whom he designed it. It was built between 1800 and 1810, and is a two-storeyed building having six towers at irregular intervals round it and four entrances which were originally drawbridges over the deep revetted moat. This is now empty of water but is believed to be in some way connected to the Gumti.

Some say that Sa'adat Ali Khan's son, Ghazi-ud-Din, completed the house on his accession to the throne and that he added the moat and drawbridges. Ornamenting the outside of the house is a frieze of suns carved in stone. An unusual feature is an inside staircase, built thus instead of outside as usual, because the house was expressly designed for women in *purdah*.

When Oudh ceased to be an independent kingdom in 1856, the Khurshaed Munzil was occupied by the officers of the regiment quartered in Lawrence Terrace, and became known to fame as the 32nd Mess House. In 1857 it was taken possession of by the insurgents and was the scene of sharp fighting.

On July 7, Havelock started from Allahabad on the first relief expedition, and by September 25 his force was within a few hundred yards of the Residency. Musketry fire assailed them from the Khurshaed Munzil as their enemies contested every foot of the way. At that time there was a more or less open field of fire between the Kaiser Bagh and the rising ground upon which stands the Khurshaed Munzil except for the maze of lanes and low-walled courtyards covering the gardens where the statue of Queen Victoria now stands.

From 9 a.m. on November 17, Peel's guns concentrated on Khurshaed Munzil and at about three in the afternoon, when the musketry fire from its defenders had diminished, Captain (afterwards Field-Marshal Viscount) Wolseley of the 90th Foot was ordered to lead an assault against it, his force consisting of a company of the 90th and detachments of the 53rd Foot and the 2nd Punjab

Infantry. The enemy failed to stand up against their concerted rush. Lieutenant (afterwards Field-Marshal Lord) Roberts closely supported by Sir David Baird and Captain Hopkins of the 53rd Foot made a dash for the narrow staircase of the turret nearest to the Kaiser Bagh, and planted there the standard of the 2nd Punjab Infantry. Twice was it shot down but the third time it resisted every effort to dislodge it and proclaimed to all and sundry the capture of the house.

By this time only four hundred yards separated the relieving force from the garrison. Outram and Havelock were determined to press on. Sir Colin Campbell was awaiting them on the sloping lawns of the Khurshaed Munzil. Hope Grant, an eye-witness of the incident, records "a cordial shaking of hands." Just inside the main entrance to the Khurshaed Munzil stands a small pillar which bears the inscription: "It was here that Havelock, Outram and Sir Colin Campbell met on the 17th November, 1857." J. Jones Barker painted a well known picture entitled "The Meeting of the Generals at the Relief of Lucknow." The original belongs to the Glasgow Municipality and a copy hangs in the museum at the Residency. Another writer describes the scene thus: "What a meeting was that ! The Iron Chief, Sir Colin, with the dust of battle still upon him, the good Sir James, and the dying Havelock. Meeting, too, while the walls of the palace where they stood were still reverberating with the din of battle—fit atmosphere for that reunion. True knights, these three brave hearts ! Each had imperilled his life to rescue the helpless, and one was soon to lay his down, worn out in their defence."

The possession of the Khurshaed Munzil was the keystone to

the whole position, and when it was once in the hands of the relieving force the relief of the Residency was assured.

Early the next year, when the British had withdrawn from their hard-won posts in Lucknow, the opposing force reoccupied them and their second line circled round the Khurshaed Munzil and the Moti Mahal.

On March 11, 1858, a British battery situated where the Colvin Institute now stands began to bombard the Khurshaed Munzil. Two days later it was recaptured for the last time.

In 1876 the Lucknow Girls' School, founded by Mrs. Abbott, moved from the Moti Mahal to the Khurshaed Munzil, and Government made over the building free of rent to the School authorities on condition that it should be returned if at any time the school were abolished. The name of the school was changed to La Martinière Girls' School because it was to enjoy some of the funds of General Martin's trust. Spacious halls form class rooms and the drawing room on the ground floor. Above are dormitories for some sixty pupils. Wide verandahs skirt the lofty rooms. From each of the six turrets one has a fine view of the surrounding country. On one of them still proudly stands a battered flagstaff.

THE LAL BARADARI

THE LAL OR RED BARADARI is so called because of the colour with which its exterior is still ornamented. It stands on the opposite side of the road to the Great Chutter Munzil and was built by Sa'adat Ali Khan between 1789 and 1814. It is sometimes known as the Qasr-us-Sultan and was built as a throne room or a coronation hall for royal durbars.

Baradari literally means a building with twelve doors, and William Knighton describes this one as it was in the reign of Nasir-ud-Din Haider who ruled fourteen years after the death of Sa'adat Ali Khan. Like every room in the palace it had suffered alterations induced by Nasir-ud-Din's obsession with the west. Rich scarlet and gold tapestry hung on the walls. A dim light filtered through the windows, enhancing the solemnity of royal receptions. A few full length portraits of the royal family hung upon the walls while the throne occupied the upper end of the hall. It was of great value and consisted of a platform approached by six steps. Three sides were protected by a golden railing. The sides were of solid silver richly ornamented with jewels. Former kings had been content to sit in oriental fashion upon a velvet cushion placed on this platform ; but Nasir-ud-Din was too westernised and insisted upon having a gold and ivory chair.

A square canopy supported by wooden poles covered with beaten gold hung above a throne ornamented with precious stones. A magnificent emerald, said to be the largest in the world, hung at the front of the canopy which was of crimson velvet with rich golden embroidery and a fringe of pearls matching the window curtains. A gilt chair stood upon the right of the throne for the Resident.

At public durbars and state councils the nobility of Oudh and English officers were presented to the King. They advanced with a present which the King touched if disposed to be very gracious, or bowed distantly to signify resentment. The prime minister took the present and laid it on one side of the throne, and the presenter retired backwards to the right or left—usually to the right if a European, to the left if an Indian. Then the King placed a necklace of honour around the neck of the Resident who returned the compliment. Then they advanced into the centre of the hall where necklaces were bestowed upon them. These necklaces were usually made of silver ribands and were worth from five to twenty-five rupees.

At the conclusion of these cremonious levees the King conducted the Resident to the door of the apartment, poured attar of roses on his hands, and exclaimed, "God be with you !" before making his way to his private apartment.

It was in the Lal Baradari that the Queen Begum tried to install on the throne her adopted grandson, Moona Jan, when Nasir-ud-Din Haider died of poison in the Farhat Baksh, a stone's throw away.

The building is now used as a museum and contains many things of interest including delicately executed portraits of men who in years gone by played a big part in the administration of the rich little kingdom of Oudh.

LA MARTINIERE

"Here lies Claude Martin, Born at Lyons, the 5th day of January, 1735. Arrived in India as a common soldier and died at Lucknow, the 13th September, 1800, a Major-General. Pray for his soul."

General Martin directed in his long and interesting will that these words should be inscribed on the tombstone which covers his remains in La Martinière College, Lucknow. They were inspired not so much by a desire for self-advertisement but as an example to future generations of schoolboys of what determination and enterprise could do.

Claude Martin was the son of a French silk manufacturer of Lyons and first came to India in 1758 in the bodyguard of the Governor of Pondicherry. A year or two later he deserted, taking with him many of his countrymen whom he formed, with the consent of the English, into a band of French chasseurs with himself at their head. This continued until 1764 when in spite of his utmost efforts his men mutinied. A few years later found him making survey maps of Oudh. He was of an inventive turn of mind and attracted the notice of the reigning Nawab, Shuja-ud-Doulah, who obtained Martin's discharge in order to entrust him with his own artillery park and arsenal.

La Martinière was originally called "Constantia" from General Martin's motto, *labore et constantia.* The ceilings are domed and in the whole building there is not a single wooden beam. The original palace consisted only of the central portion and is of curious design, many of the rooms being linked half way up the walls by a circular purdah gallery so that in very truth the walls might have ears. The curved wings were built about 1840, in accordance with the General's will which was written with scrupulous care in triplicate in both English and Urdu. The pillar standing in the lake was also built under the terms of his will as memorial. The lake originally covered a much smaller area and was enlarged in 1880 as a famine relief measure.

The artist Zoffany was an Oudh contemporary of Martin's.

In the very room through which she must so often have passed, hangs a picture by Zoffany of one of General Martin's wives. She was of a princely family from which she ran way, to be discovered, by a French officer in the *chikan* work bazar in Lucknow. He bought her and sold her again to General Martin at the age of about eight. He educated her and finally married her. In this painting she is portrayed with one of Martin's adopted sons.

The ceilings of all the rooms in La Martinière are in the bas-relief Italian style of raised plaster work in green, blue and pink. At intervals real wedgewood plaques are pegged into the walls, some only an inch or two in diameter and others about two feet by three, numbering some hundreds in each room.

Below the ground level in the *tykhana* General Martin lies buried. This is according to his directions, in order to prevent the building from being appropriated by Mussalmans. In pre-Mutiny days figures of French grenadiers, their arms reversed, guarded the tomb. The rebels broke these and even scattered General Martin's bones to the four winds. When peace was restored they were collected and reinstated, but the statues were lost for all time. General Martin designed a most ingenious air cooling system. Great pillars run at intervals from top to bottom of the building. Down the centre of each is driven an air shaft with holes communicating with the various rooms through which it passes, thus enabling the hot air to rise and the cool air to take its place.

The school boasts a fine library which adjoins the chapel. Both must originally have been reception rooms. In the latter are some good stained glass windows and memorial slabs. One of these is to Captain Spence who for 64 years was connected with La Martinière. He came as a foundationer and ultimately became the estate superintendent. The estate covers an area of roughly two square miles. He left a substantial sum of money to the College when he died, which contributed largely to the Spence Hall.

An old-fashioned cannon named "The Lord Cornwallis" stands on the terrace. It was cast in 1786 by Martin who actually accompanied it to Seringapatam in 1792. In 1871 it was restored to the College by the Allahabad Arsenal. He also cast a large bell which he intended for use as a school bell. After the Mutiny it was found cracked and half buried in the garden. Some fifteen years ago it was restored and set in its place.

Huge stone lions adorn the upper terrace of the building; in their heads are spaces intended for lanterns whose beams would gleam out between the teeth of the monsters. At the corners are little turrets loop-holed every few inches. Still higher, statues adorn the terrace balustrades. Above the third storey a flagstaff stands on the crest of an enormous crown, which commands a glorious view of the city and the surrounding country.

During the insurrection the sixty-five boys of La Martinière withdrew to the Residency, where the Martinière Post was garrisoned by the teachers and bigger boys under the command of Mr. George Schilling, the Principal of the School. Mrs. Bartrum mentions in her diary the "little servants" who acted as messengers, and who were the younger boys of La Martinière. During the entire siege only three boys were wounded ; two died from disease.

On November 14 at 9 a.m., Sir Colin Campbell's force started from the Alam Bagh on their relief march. Until they neared Dilkusha no resistance was offered them for they had come by an unsuspected route, but there they were met by musketry and artillery fire. This they soon overcame. Pushing on they rapidly drove the rebels out of La Martinière at the point of the bayonet and by noon were in position.

Since those troublous times only the high floods of 1915 and 1923 have disturbed the even tenor of this famous school.

THE MACHHI BHAWAN

ALTHOUGH ALL TRACE HAS long since vanished of any part of the actual Machhi Bhawan fort, the name lingers and applies to the mound upon which the Medical Colleges now stand.

In 1470 A.D. a Muhammadan saint named Sheikh Mina was born at Lucknow. He was educated by an eminent dervish,

Quiran-ud-Din. At his death a tomb was erected over his remains. It is carefully preserved to this day and is the oldest identified monument in Lucknow. It is a place of pilgrimage.

The city in those days was known as Lukshmanpur. When Mahmud of Ghazni invaded India he brought with him Sheikhs and Pathans some of whom settled in Lukshmanpur.

A Hindu architect name Likhna designed a fort for them known as Likhna Kila which gradually shortened into Lucknow. Within its sheltering walls stood the Panch Mahal, so called because it was five storeys high. When Sa'adat Khan first moved his court from Fyzabad to Lucknow in 1732 he hired the Panch Mahal and another building known as the Mubarak Mahal for about five hundred and fifty rupees a month. Then Nawab Safdar Jang came to the throne in 1739. He strengthened the fortifications of the old fort and renamed it Machhi Bhawan, or Fish House, "machhi" meaning fish and "bhawan" being the Sanskrit word for house. He enlarged it to reach the river. High walls encompassed it. From the water it looked like a fortress commanding the old stone bridge now swept away. On the south-east side it overlooked the Residency. Beneath the outer walls ran the most frequented thoroughfares of the city.

Asaf-ud-Doulah, the fourth Nawab, who succeeded to the throne in 1775 and is generally acknowledged to have been the greatest of the rulers of Oudh, strengthened the fort still more with round earthen bastions. Within he built a palace facing the Gumti, consisting of six main quadrangles surrounded by pavilions. Entrance was by two noble gateways, the outer one containing the Naubat Khana where musicians played at stated times every day.

The state apartments encompassed the main courtyard in the centre of which was a well. Fountains played and streams wound in and out to keep it cool during the summer.

In 1784 the Great Imambara was built as a famine relief measure within the Machhi Bhawan area—which gives some slight idea of the size of the fortress.

In 1857 the buildings within the fort were the property of Nawab Yahuja Ali Khan who sold them to Sir Henry Lawrence for Rs. 50,000. Murmurs of unrest were even then beginning to be heard, so Sir Henry gave orders that the fortifications of the Machhi Bhawan should be strengthened. By the middle of May he was prepared for all eventualities and had distributed his troops. To the Machhi Bhawan he sent a hundred Europeans, three hundred sepoys and about twenty guns, with a large quantity of ammunition. On the last day of May he hastily transferred his headquarters to the Lucknow Residency from Mariaon and feverishly fortified the surrounding positions. Cellars were excavated and ammunition from the Machhi Bhawan stored in them. Preparations went on more or less unimpeded until news was brought that the advance guard of a force from Nawabgunj had already reached Chinhut and was preparing to advance on Lucknow.

At sunset on June 29, British troops quietly withdrew with their entourage into the Residency and the Machhi Bhawan; on the 30th a force of six hundred and eighty-six men and eleven guns advanced to the disastrous battle of Chinhut. The little force was badly defeated. It was forced to retire but held its own until the guns from the Machhi Bhawan checked the oncoming enemy, enabling it to withdraw into the Residency.

The guns from the fort prevented the enemy from crossing by the stone bridge, but early in June the river dwindled until it was fordable and they made their way across into houses overlooking the Residency from which they proceeded to pour musketry fire into the British position.

Thus the siege began.

At daybreak on July 1 the besiegers made their first attack on the Residency. It was repulsed, but Sir Henry came to the conclusion that there were not enough troops to defend both positions, so a semaphore was sent from the Residency to the Machhi Bhawan saying, "Spike the guns well, blow up the fort, and retire at midnight." At that hour, then, the defenders of the fort, commanded by Colonel Palmer, marched into the Residency with guns and treasure, leaving two hundred and forty barrels of gunpowder, which blew up with a terrible explosion a few minutes later, a train of gunpowder having been laid by Captain M. C. Thomas of the Madras Artillery.

Mrs. Bartrum records in her diary: "Last night the Machhi Bhawan fort was blown up. It was such a tremendous shock that we all sprung out of our beds....thinking that the sepoys had really blown up our defences and forced their way in. Our room was so thick in dust that when we had lighted a candle we could scarce see one another.

The next morning a voice outside the Water Gate of the Residency was heard shouting, "Arrah, then, open your gates." The speaker was a private of the 32nd Regiment, who had been drunk the night before and asleep when the evacuation took place. He had been blown up—which rapidly sobered him—but he was unhurt. The force of the explosion had torn every stitch of clothing off him and he arrived at the Residency stark naked.

Nothing more is heard of the fort until early the following year, when on March 16 Outram's force captured it after slight resistance. The same year it was rebuilt and after being strongly fortified was occupied by troops and officers' families.

In 1905 when King George V visited India as Prince of Wales, he came to Lucknow in December and laid the foundation-stone of the Medical College. In January 1912, Sir John Prescott performed the opening ceremony of the buildings now known as King George's and Queen Mary's Medical Colleges.

THE MAQBARA OF AMJAD ALI SHAH

KING Amjad Ali Shah came to the throne of Oudh in 1842. He reigned until he died on February 13, 1847 "of an ulcer, or some such sore on his shoulder, and.....the sore must have been poisoned by some one, most probably by one of the physicians bribed by some one who benefited most by his death....When the King, Amjad Ali

Shah, felt his end approaching, he ordered the council-chamber to be prepared and fresh carpets to be spread, and new cushions, and he had his beard trimmed, and put on new and splendid clothing and, having lain down in the council-chamber, he sent for the queen. There they both wept, and he spoke much to her in whispers. The boil or ulcer on his shoulder at that time was as large as a saucer, and the flesh all eaten away, it was said, from some poisonous ointment given by the physician. How can I tell if the report was true? Such was the rumour in the palace, and of course the physician would not have dared to do so of himself. He must have been bribed to do it.

"After much whispering talk he said he would sleep, and the queen laid down his head gently and covered it. The attendants, suspecting he was dead, got her away with great difficulty and she thought he was still sleeping; but he was dead. He died, like a king, in his royal robes on his throne, in his council-chamber."

When the King was dead, the sound of wailing was drowned in the shouts of gladness proclaiming the new King Wajid Ali Shah. The Queen mother was forced to abandon her dead, to clothe herself in gorgeous raiment and attend the coronation of her son. The body was left to the care of servants who prepared it for burial within the dark and silent palace. From without came the noise of joy and commotion, cannons firing and bands playing.

Amjad Ali Shah died early in the morning. The coronation ceremony, when the court lords took the oath of allegiance, lasted until past midnight. When the poor widowed queen was at last permitted to return to the palace, she found her lord and master already buried. He lies in the Imambara which faces Hazrat Ganj, near Mission Road and the Lal Bagh, shielded from view by a large gateway.

The building has little architectural beauty. It is a single rectangular chamber approached by a fine flight of steps. At the top of them a stone tank abuts on to a stone terrace for ablutions of the faithful.

Shabby doors fitted with broken panes of glass afford a glimpse of the interior now furnished with little but cobwebs. Once this was lavishly lined with silken carpets, wonderful chandeliers and priceless art treasures, but during the troubles of 1857 the local hooligans could not withstand the attractions of loot. They stripped the Imambara of everything of value. Beneath a trap-door in the centre of the floor a few steps lead to the vault where the King's body lies, forgotten and forsaken.

On March 12 and 13, 1858, after the Begum Kothi had been taken, the British troops pushed on to Amjad Ali Shah's tomb from which they drove their enemies with the help of a couple of batteries of guns, which made two breaches in the south-eastern wall of the Imambara enclosure. Two companies of the 10th Foot and about a hundred men of the Ferozpore Sikhs formed a storming party. Feeble resistance was offered and the troops pressed on to an outlying building of the Kaiser Bagh Palaces.

When Oudh became quiet this Imambara was used as the English Church until 1860 when Christ Church was completed. Lord Canning during his second visit to Lucknow attended divine service in the building.

Christ Church was built as a memorial to those who lost their lives as a result of the Mutiny. Its walls bear many brass tablets recalling names and places associated with unparalleled bravery. The Reverend Henry Polehampton, with his infant son, is here remembered: he was severely wounded whilst shaving and later succumbed to an attack of cholera. Nawab Mohin-ud-Doulah Bahadur of Lucknow erected a tablet to Captain Maclean of the 7th Regiment, Native Infantry, as a token of his friendship and regard. The great Kavanagh who took his life in his own hands "with the devotion of an ancient Roman", and Major Johnson, who had been through the Crimean and Persian campaigns—these and many others are remembered in the quiet and peaceful Church.

In the earthquake of 1933, the Cross on the spire of the Church was twisted until it faced down Hazrat Gunj.

THE MAQBARA OF SA'ADAT ALI KHAN

CONTRARY TO CUSTOM, NAWAB Sa'adat Ali Khan did not build his own tomb; for the place where it stands with that of his wife Khurshaed Zadi, overlooking the present Oudh Gymkhana Club tennis courts, was formerly the site of a royal palace.

Before Sa'adat Ali Khan came to the throne in 1798 he lived for some years in Calcutta and adopted many European customs and ideas, among them a belief in the merits of the East India Company.

Asaf-ud-Doulah died in 1797 leaving no legitimate heir. A claimant who pretended to be his son was actually allowed to sit on the throne for four months until the British deposed him in favour of Sa'adat Ali Khan, half brother to Asaf-ud-Doulah. The latter did much to beautify his capital with palaces, mosques and bridges, to the detriment of the state coffers which suffered still more from the lavish splendour in which the Nawab lived. On the accession of Sa'adat Ali Khan life in the capital proceeded as usual, and the Nawab continued to indulge his extravagant tastes, paying no attention to the duties incumbent upon him. Lord Wellesley was then Governor-General and he decided that the Nawab's army must be disbanded. Financial difficulties became more and more acute and in November 1801, by the Treaty of Lucknow, the Nawab relinquished all claim to ten districts receiving in return British assistance for internal and external defence.

At the same time he made a vow at the shrine of Hazrat Abbas to devote himself thereafter wholly to the welfare of his state. Colonel Sleeman, Resident at Lucknow from 1849-56, says that he kept his vow, and no King of Oudh ever conducted the Government with so much ability as he did for the remaining fourteen years of his life. As late as 1880, "he was still remembered, even by the large landholders—to keep whom in check was one of his chief aims—as the best, wisest and strongest administrator the province ever knew."

He gained an unmerited reputation for parsimony and extortionate dealings, probably because he employed Europeans to cope with refractory zamindars and did not allow the enormous and useless expenditure usual in an eastern state.

He had nine sons. For his favourite wife, Khurshaed Zadi, he built the Khurshaed Munzil, now the Martinière Girls' School, as well as many other fine buildings including Dilkusha Palace and the Moti Mahal. In spite of this he cleared his kingdom of debt. At his death fourteen crores of rupees constituted a reserve treasury.

On July 11, 1814 Sa'adat Ali Khan died and was succeeded by his son Ghazi-ud-Din Haider. The latter announced that as he had taken his father's place, his father must have his. In accordance with this somewhat astonishing reasoning, he pulled down his palace and built instead his father's tomb on the site. It is a fine conception although its proportions have since been spoilt by a grass mound piled around its foot. From the base of the dome the panorama of Lucknow unfolds itself to the bold adventurer who decides to risk the cracks produced by a recent earthquake.

The floor is paved with squares of black and white marble. A marked depression running from north to south indicates the King's last resting place. The tomb proper flanked by those of his two brothers, lies in a vault beneath and is reached by a dark and narrow winding stair. In the same building lie three of his wives and three daughters. His favourite wife, Khurshaed Zadi, mother of Ghazi-ud-Din Haider, is buried a stone's throw away in a similar mausoleum slightly smaller than his own.

During the Mutiny both tombs were strongly fortified with concealed cannon which effected considerable damage to Havelock's force during the first relief. On March 13, 1858 Frank's column occupied the courtyard of the tombs and, from the scant shelter it afforded, stormed the Kaiser Bagh.

In their hurried flight from Lucknow early in 1858, the rebels abandoned near the Jama Masjid a number of tin boxes and leather cases containing gunpowder. General Outram ordered the sappers to destroy them and so, on March 17, under the direction of Captain Clerke, Adjutant of the Royal Engineers, they conveyed them to a large and deep well and began to throw them down. One of the boxes scraped the side of the well and blew up, igniting box after box, until the whole exploded, killing Captain Clerke, Lieutenant Brownlow of the Bengal Engineers, a corporal, a lance-corporal and twelve sappers of the 23rd Company of Royal Engineers. A flat marble slab surrounded by a low iron railing marks the spot of this disaster a few yards from the resting places of Sa'adat Ali Khan and his wife. So a Muhammadan eastern potentate lies cheek by jowl with such sturdy British yeomen as Sapper Andrew Fairservice, Sapper James Bunting and Sapper John Yeo.

THE MARIAON CANTONMENT IN THE EIGHTEEN FIFTIES

BETWEEN THE third and fourth milestone on the road leading from Lucknow to Sitapur, about a hundred yards from the left hand side, there stands an obelisk—all that remains of what was once a large and flourishing cantonment.

Many years before the cantonment existed, an ascetic named Mandal Rikh lived in a great forest. The place where he dwelt became known as Mandiaon. For a long time it was peopled by the Bhar tribe eventually driven out by one of Saiyid Salar's Lieutenants, Malik Adam, who in his turn was killed and buried in the Subhatia Mohalla of Lucknow. About a hundred and fifty years later Raja Singh conquered the village and made it over to his Kayasth and Brahmin followers whose descendants live there to this day.

When Sa'adat Ali Khan came to the throne in 1798, he built a cantonment called Mariaon for the European community which flourished during the 19th century. There were lines for three native infantry regiments, a battery of European horse artillery and a bullock battery of regular native artillery. At Mudkipur, a couple of miles away, were the 7th Light Cavalry.

A little way down the Lucknow-Sitapur road stands a large house with semi-circular gates—the few remaining traces of a rich Nawab's house. On either side of each gate stood a cage, one containing a fine tiger, the other three or four small leopards. Begging at the gate near by sat an old Mussalman Fakir, naked except for a cloth round his loins.

A little further along the road, on the left-hand side, is the shed of another big house, still called "Beechy Sahib ka Bangala" by the villagers. Here it was that the Reverend Henry Polehampton lived with his wife. Mr. Polehampton, in one of his long and interesting letters, says: "I think I told you long ago, they say this houso is haunted..and that no one but a Padre can live in it. They say Mr. Beechy who died there haunts it." In those days it had the best garden in cantonments, with plenty of strawberries, oranges and lemons and quantities of other fruit trees, vegetables, and flowers.

Life in cantonments then was very much as it is now, only cheaper. The "Khansama" or house-steward was paid ten rupees a month ; a "khitmutgar" or table-attendant seven ; the dhobi, ayah, cook and bearer, eight each ; bhisti, sweeper, chowkidar and palanquin bearers four each ; punkah coolies, gardeners, and grass cutters three ; and the goat boy one. The average rent was about sixty pounds. Board and lodging and servants came to about £280 per annum.

The Polehamptons kept six or seven goats and every evening and morning, before tea and breakfast, they were milked just outside the verandah and the milk came in foaming. Most of the servants were married. Altogether there were fifty children in the compound. The servants' houses were built of earth and were low and dark.

There was an ice club and a book club. The subscription to the latter was heavy, but then everything English was expensive and books were badly needed. They had wood fires for there was no such thing as coal, wood costing in the bazaar a rupee for three maunds. They had to depend a good deal upon local products for food, such as custard apples and Indian corn grown in the garden which they roasted for dessert ; and green young lemons.

The church was near the Polehamptons' house and held about a hundred people. A little distance away along a broad metalled road was the cemetery shaded by fine trees. The route, now inches deep in sand, may still be seen leading off the main road to the right and passing through a village on the site of the old Bullock Battery lines.

A little beyond the village lies the graveyard, a sorry sight of dilapidated tombs. Trees have thrust their limbs between the masonry. Head stones lurch drunkenly at a precarious angle. Only two lead inscriptions have escaped the pillagers' hands, those of Lieutenants MacDonnell and Richards. The former was the Adjutant of the 2nd Punjab Cavalry, and was killed in action at Courci in March 1858. The enemy were in retreat, but they showed indomitable courage when the British troopers charged through them three times. They never even wavered. During these charges MacDonnell was killed and Captain Cosserat of the 34th Madras Light Infantry, then in command of a squadron of the 1st Punjab Cavalry, was wounded. He lingered on for over a fortnight, being laid to rest in the Residency Cemetery. Lieutenant Richards took part in the attack on Birwa Fort in Hardoi, carried out by Brigadier Barker as late as October 1858. He was wounded there and brought back to die early in December at Mariaon.

Although disease and epidemic carried away a large percentage of the population, life was not all funerals and Mariaon boasted a fine park. Dinner at three was "tiffin" to fashionable Anglo-Indians who dined at eight. A band of one of the regiments played every evening at sunset for about an hour. Gentlemen would get out of their buggies and go about talking to ladies at their carriage doors. At about seven they all went home.

All that remains of the Mariaon Residency are the foundations upon which has been erected an obelisk. Affixed to it is a plaque which reads :—

"This pillar commemorates old Mariaon cantonment garrisoned in 1857 by the 13th, 48th and 71st Native Infantry. A large proportion of the regiments mutinied on the evening of May 30, 1857. This pillar marks the site of the Residency Bungalow occupied by Sir Henry Lawrence, K.C.B., on that memorable occasion and subsequently by rebels. The mutiny of May 30 was crushed by a small force of British and loyal Indian troops, and the rebels were routed, but the Mariaon cantonment was abandoned on the 29th June, 1857, when Sir Henry Lawrence's force concentrated on the Lucknow Residency and the Machi Bhawan."

Sir Henry refers to the Mariaon Residency in one of his letters as being nearly as large as his town house in Lucknow.

On May 18, 1857, Sir Henry wrote: "Time is everything just now—time, firmness, promptness, conciliation, and prudence.... ten men may in an hour quell a row which after a day's delay may take weeks to put down."

False alarms of risings were rife. Sir Henry took no notice of a rumour that a rising was timed to begin at 9 p.m. on May 30. That evening some officers on his staff were dining with him at the Mariaon Residency. After dinner they strolled out on to the verandah. When the 9 o'clock gun fired, Sir Henry said smilingly, "Your friends are not punctual." Scarcely had he said it when there was a burst of musketry and fires were seen burning in all directions. Hastily the horses were saddled and Sir Henry and his staff rode off to the camp of the 32nd Regiment where the men were already drawn up for action together with the European battery.

Almost immediately the sepoys of the 71st Native Infantry appeared and began firing upon the 32nd, but they fled when the English troops retaliated. In their flight they murdered

Lieutenant Grant commanding a picket in cantonments.

In spite of patrols the mutineers pillaged and looted all night, Brigadier Handscomb being killed by a chance bullet.

Only the Residency escaped the attention of the insurgents. Next morning it was estimated that about seven hundred men had remained faithful from the three native infantry regiments and the 7th Light Cavalry. At Mudkipur the men had burnt and sacked the Cavalry lines. Cornet Raleigh, a boy of seventeen, had been sick in quarters in Mudkipur: when attemping to mount his horse that morning, he was killed without a chance to defend himself.

The troops remained in Mariaon while Sir Henry transferred his headquarters to the Lucknow Residency. When everything was ready the entire European population withdrew behind the walls of the Machhi Bhawan and the Residency. The famous siege had begun!

THE MOTI MAHAL

THE MOTI MAHAL, OR PEARL Palace, was thus called because its original dome resembled a pearl. It has been through many vicissitudes since then and was re-roofed in 1923. The name now embraces two other erstwhile famous buildings, the Mubarak Manzil and the Shah Manzil. The Moti Mahal was built by Nawab Sa'adat Ali Khan between 1798 and 1814. The other two were added by his son and successor Ghazi-ud-Din Haider. They are now the property of the Maharaja of Balrampur.

The royal fish badge ornaments the entrance gateway, from which a wide drive leads between gay flower beds to the Moti Mahal itself. Here at the Mubarak Munzil fights of large animals took place, generally in a special enclosure where stood a balcony for the King and his attendants.

In 1856 an excellent road with lamp posts on either side led to the Shah Munzil, a spacious palace stretching to the Gumti. It had a lovely garden where lemon and orange trees mingled with rose and pomegranate. Fountains and statues adorned the garden where gold and silver fish gavotted.

On September 25, 1857, the relief column under Havelock took a route unforeseen by the enemy. After sharp skirmishing around the area of the Yellow House, they proceeded unmolested until they reached the Moti Mahal where there was some heavy fighting. Guns from the Kaiser Bagh and the Khurshaed Munzil took toll of them until they reached the lee of the Chutter Munzil. They ejected the garrison of the Moti Mahal and left the wounded there together with the heavy guns and ammunition under the command of Colonel Robert P. Campbell of the 90th Perthshire Light Infantry. Their protection proved insufficient and the whole of the next day had to be spent in extricating them. Colonel Campbell got out the next night but was shot in the knee, his leg being later amputated. He could not withstand the shock and died, and is commemorated with the other officers and men of the 90th Perthshire Light Infantry in the Residency Cemetery.

On that day, September 26, Brigadier Cooper of the Artillery and Dr. Bartrum were both killed in the courtyard of the Moti Mahal. At the outbreak of the Mutiny Dr. Bartrum with his wife and child was at Ghonda, about 80 miles from Lucknow. By June 6, Mrs. Bartrum says that they were becoming alarmed. The next day Sir Henry Lawrence sent a messenger *via* Secrora, ordering the ladies and children into Lucknow for better security, Mrs. Bartrum and her baby were confined within the Residency during the siege and on September 23 she wrote, "Such joyful news! A letter is come from Sir James Outram in which he says we shall be relieved in a few days ; every one is wild with excitement and joy. Can it really be true?"

Three days later, the very day her husband was killed, she was up with daylight and dressed her baby in the one clean dress which she had kept for him throughout the siege until his father should come. The next day, she was still watching for her husband and still he came not. On the 28th the servants brought in a few things belonging to him. His sword, his pistol, and his instrument case had all been taken. The grief-stricken widow recognised her dead husband's horse.

During the second relief, when the rebels had been driven out of the Khurshaed Munzil, they were pursued to the Moti Mahal with desperate bayonet fighting, when the British force gradually drove their opponents from room to room and finally stood panting in sole possession.

A garden path still clings to the original garden wall and leads to a stone erected in 1932 stating, "This tablet commemorates the reuniting of the two wings of the 90th Perthshire Light Infantry, now the 2nd Battalion, the Cameronians (Scottish Rifles), near this spot during the relief of the Residency, 17th November, 1857." Another, visible from Clyde Road, says that "About 20 paces from this spot in the side wall of the Moti Mahal was the gap through which Sir James Outram and Sir Henry Havelock passed on their way to meet Sir Colin Campbell when the relieved and relieving forces joined hands on the 17th November, 1857." This historic reunion in the garden of the Khurshaed Munzil has been commemorated in a famous picture, "The Meeting of the Generals."

THE MUSA BAGH

FURTHER AFIELD THAN MOST OF Lucknow's historic spots lies the Musa Bagh. The effort of finding it is well rewarded by the calm and peaceful atmosphere of the old house, as it reigns supreme over the green and fertile fields stretching on every side. From the Great Imambara, go through the Rumi Darwaza past the Husainabad Imambara and straight on. The local inhabitants are, for once, well informed of its whereabouts. After one or two vicissitudes, and remembering to go in the direction of the water works, you come suddenly upon a wide straight road, wider than the Hazratganj, once shaded by lofty trees. Upon a commanding site stand the remains of a wall weather-beaten into that beautiful colour which only old brick-work can attain. The site was originally chosen and laid out as a garden by Asaf-ud-Doulah who transferred the seat of government from Fyzabad to Lucknow in 1775. His half-brother Sa'adat Ali Khan succeeded him and built a house at one corner of the Musa Bagh.

Designed by General Claud Martin on the lines of an English country manor, it was badly knocked about in 1858, but it is possible to reconstruct it in some measure in the mind's eye. In the centre, a large hall stood supported by two noble columns of pillars from which other rooms gave off. At each corner was a small circular chamber containing a winding stair. In the centre chamber, curiously enough, a small well penetrates deep into the ground. Little of interior decoration remains except some weather-beaten stucco work touched here and there with faded colouring. A Mr. Sherer alludes to the "effigies of Nasur-ud-Din Haider" which adorned the walls of the Musa Bagh.

Oval holes cut in the high wall encircling the garden look over the fields sloping gently to the Gumti, and from this vantage point the Nawab-Wazir would watch wild beast fights whose fame had spread over all Oudh.

The contests between the smaller animals such as antelopes took place at the Musa Bagh. These animals were caught in the lower hills of the Himalayas and trained to fight. The two deer would trot towards each other, manœuvring for position, crossing their antlers, retreating and advancing until their antlers became interlocked and each antelope strained his whole frame to press his adversary backwards. At last one animal would show signs of strain and inch by inch the stronger opponent would gain ground. On pushed the stronger antelope, head depressed, every muscle starting, every limb dancing with animation, whilst his opponent rolled his eyes wildly, becoming paralysed with terror. His graceful limbs twitched with fear as he yielded ground.

Finally they reached the limit of the enclosure; still the remorseless enemy would push with renewed vigour. Resistance finally broke and the oppressed antelope turned sideways as if to escape by flight. In a moment the sharp points of the victor's antlers plunged into the flanks of the vanquished. The animal thus gored groaned with pain as he sank down, big tears coursing down his cheeks. Again and again he would try to escape, but there was no hope. Finally the stronger antelope, watching his opportunity would rush at his adversary and plunge his blood-tipped horns into the flanks of his exhausted stag which fell never to rise again.

Strangely enough the great insurrection of 1857-58 both began and ended at the Musa Bagh. The 7th Oudh Irregular Cavalry were stationed there. Having been told that a type of newly issued cartridge had been greased with cow's fat, they refused to bite it. Sir Henry Lawrence issued an order that they were to be deprived of their arms, and then events began to move. The scene of action left the Musa Bagh until March 1858, when the Queen Mother and her son took up their headquarters there with a force of some nine thousand men commanded by prominent leaders. Sir Colin Campbell naturally decided that they must not be allowed to remain there and on March 19 at 6-30 in the morning, Outram moved off towards the Musa Bagh. His force consisted of two squadrons of the 9th Lancers, Middleton's Field Battery, three companies of the 20th, seven companies of the 23rd, the 79th Highlanders, and the 2nd Punjab Infantry, supported by Hope Grant's guns and musketry fire from the opposite side of the river.

At the same time Brigadier Campbell advanced from the Alam Bagh and cut off the retreat of the flying rebels. But he was late and although his force pursued the rebels for some distance a great number of them slipped through to Fyzabad.

Captain Wale raised and commanded the 1st Sikh Irregular Cavalry and he and his regiment were among the pursuing force. After several r iles, however, he gave the order to halt. "Then from the far side of a ravine, a solitary figure fired his musket at a group of officers," killing Captain Wale. He was the eighth son of General Wale, out of a family of sixteen, and lies buried in the Musa Bagh, under a stone erected by Captain L. B. Jones, Acting-Commandant, 1st Sikh Irregular Cavalry, "as a token of regard for his officer, whom he admired both as a friend and a soldier. Captain Wale lived and died a Christian soldier."

Captain W. Heley Hutchinson and Sergeant Newman, both of the 9th Royal Lancers, were badly wounded while pursuing the enemy from Musa Bagh and both lie buried in the Wilayati Bagh When the rebels had finally been driven from the Musa Bagh by sharp fighting, a small force was detailed to occupy it, and at Lotan Bagh nearby lies Major John Griffith Price, 2nd Dragoon

Guards (Queen's Bays), who died of fever at the Musa Bagh, on the 12th of May, 1858. This force was soon withdrawn, and but for an occasional intrusion the Musa Bagh is given over to peaceful tillers of the soil.

QADAM RASUL

IN THE HORTICULTURAL GARDENS opposite the Carlton Hotel stands a small domed building upon a high artificial mound, known as the Qadam Rasul. Qadam means a step. It was erected during the reign of Nasir-ud-Din Haider, between 1827 and 1837, to house a sacred relic, an impress of the Prophet's foot in stone brought by a pilgrim from Arabia.

During the Mutiny the relic was removed, and the native forces, wishing to outwit the British, used the Qadam Rasul as a powder magazine. The besieged force incurred heavy losses from snipers stationed in mosques overlooking the Residency, which mosques the engineers wished to destroy. Sir Henry Lawrence was adamant in his reply: "Spare the holy places, and private property, too, as much as possible." The mutineers knew the respect that the British had for religious places and trusted in this to keep intact their powder magazine.

During the second relief, the fierce battle of the Sikandar Bagh was fought on November 16. After a short rest the relieving force advanced towards the Residency, but they had only gone about four hundred yards when they met with resistance from the Qadam Rasul. Standing on a mound, it looked formidable, but the nerve of its handful of defenders had been badly shaken by the fate of their comrades at the Sikandar Bagh, and the position was easily taken by the 2nd Punjab Infantry, part of Greathead's brigade.

Early the next year many posts had to be retaken. On March 11, Medley and Lang, two engineers, went on a personal reconnaissance. They found the Qadam Rasul and the Shah Najaf empty, so they called up their men and ordered them to throw up defences and earthworks so that when Sir E. Lugard advanced he was able to seize them both without opposition.

The building has been condemned as unsafe, but a flight of steps leads to the top which affords an unexpectedly good view of the Khurshaed Munzil. It is still possible to make one's way round the outside of the cracked and crumbling dome.

ROSHAN-UD-DOULAH KOTHI

THE ROSHAN-UD-Doulah Kothi lies behind the Kaiser Bagh quadrangle.

Approaching from Hazratganj, turn into the road leading down the centre of the Kaiser Bagh, go beneath the centre gateway on the right and turn immediately to the left. The Roshan-ud-Doulah confronts you.

Roshan-ud-Doulah who built it was minister to King Nasir-ud-Din Haider after the dismissal of the great reformer Hakim Mehdi in August, 1832. At that time the salary of the prime minister was Rs. 25,000 a month. Over and above this he took five per cent. of the revenue, which made his picking about six lakhs a year.

Roshan-ud-Doulah possessed a wily mind and a smooth tongue. He resented the power wielded by Europeans at Court.

One day he suggested to the King that they showed lack of respect when they entered the royal presence without removing their shoes, hoping by this means to bring them into disfavour. The King was equal to him.

"Roshan-ud-Doulah," said he, "am I a greater man than the King of England ?"

"It is not for your majesty's servant to say that anyone is greater than his lord."

"Listen to me, Nawab, and you, General, listen to me. The King of England is my master and these gentlemen would go into his presence with their shoes on. Shall they not come into mine, then ? Do they come before me with their hats on ? Answer me, Your Excellency."

"They do not, Your Majesty."

"No, that is *their* way of showing respect. *They* take off their hats, and *you* take off your shoes. But, come now, let us have a bargain. Wallah, but I will get them to take off their shoes and leave them without, as you do, if you will take off your turban and leave it without, as they do."

The Nawab said never another word,

The King and his minister would disguise themselves in European clothes and wander about the bazaars, listening to the general conversations after the manner of the caliphs of ancient Baghdad.

Some years later the Roshan-ud-Doulah Kothi was turned into Government offices, which function it still fills. The lofty centre chamber is filled with clerks sitting cross-legged at their little sloping desks a few inches high. Through many rooms and up a narrow winding stair is a flat roof. There perches a little iron statue of a famous dacoit, which was slightly injured by the earthquake of 1933.

This dacoit performed many deeds of daring. So cunning was he that the authorities could never catch him. One day he sent a message to say that he would visit the Roshan-ud-Doulah Kothi on a certain date at a certain time. Many were the preparations and traps set to catch him, but he evaded them and paid his call in safety. He was never caught to the day of his death, and to his memory this iron statue was erected.

Roshan-ud-Doulah also built the Qaiser Pasand which occupies a similar position to the Roshan-ud-Doulah Kothi on the opposite side of the Kaiser Bagh.

After the death of Nasir-ud-Din Haider Wajid Ali Shah confiscated it and gave it to his favourite concubine, Mashuq-us-Sultan.

In 1857, some of the refugees from Sitapur were captured and confined to the lower rooms of the Qaiser Pasand, where they were comparatively well treated until their captors were repulsed from an attack upon the Alam Bagh. On September 24, they were dragged out and murdered in a nullah not far from the gate of the Chini Bazaar upon Neill Road, where a memorial has since been raised.

Somewhere between the Roshan-ud-Doulah and the Qaiser Pasand a giant mulberry tree spread its shade over a marble platform.

Once a year the Kaiser Bagh was thrown open to the public for a great fair. The trunk of the mulberry tree was then painted a vivid scarlet. Upon the marble platform sat King Wajid Ali Shah dressed in the saffron robes of a fakir, while his subjects streamed past him. Besides the more humble pleasure seekers, "mounted cavaliers in rich clothes, embroidered with gold, preceded by attendants carrying gold and silver sticks, swords, spears and wands of office, passed to and fro in a continuous stream. Dignitaries seated in open palanquins richly painted and gilded, mingled with the throng, followed by armed retainers and mounted escort, others reclined gracefully in curved howdahs, some of which were of silver, upon the backs of elephants.

THE RUMI DARWAZA

Beyond the Great Imambara and at right angles to it stands the Rumi Darwaza, or Turkish Gate which turns its finest architectural face to Husainabad. From the Great Imambara it is seen as a massive structure with a tiny aperture in the base to admit the traffic. The best view is obtaind by driving about a hundred yards beyond, until a road leads left to Victoria Park. There turn round and look at the gateway.

It is the half of a vast dome cut perpendicularly, lavishly encrusted with ornamentations. Against the sky stands a frieze of knobs suggesting, so it is said, the heads of malefactors placed there by way of warning to their friends.

The gateway was built in 1784 at the same time as the Great Imambara at the instance of Asaf-ud-Doulah. It was relief work during the great famine which lasted from 1784 to 1786. Tradition says that it is a copy of the Porte Sublime in Istambul. No gateway of like design exists there to-day although there may have been one before 1453, when Muhammad II conquered the city. Gate and Imambara harmonise with each other.

Just beyond the Rumi Darwaza a low white wall surrounds rising ground shaded by trees. In this peaceful spot lie buried those who dwelt and died in the Machhi Bhawan when it had been rebuilt after its destruction in 1857. It was the fashion at that period to indulge in flights of poetic fancy, though the final results do not always inspire the emotion intended by the author.

Over the remains of Sergeant Lawrence Byrne, his loving wife states in jaunty measure—

"Passing stranger call it not
A place of dreary gloom.
I love to linger near the spot
It is my husband's tomb."

—which cannot surely have been quite the impression she intended to convey.

Another occupant of a tomb, Gunner Martin, complacently

says in the course of a lengthy verse –

> "I know you felt it hard to part
> With me the darling of your heart."

They are not all in this strain. One pathetic stone was raised by the parents of four children, three of whom died at the age of two and a half, while the fourth struggled on only to die when she was eight.

Opposite the gate of this little graveyard a road runs down one side of the Husainabad Garden. A little way beyond this, on the left hand side, is another tiny cemetery, badly overgrown and in a sorry state of disrepair. In it are ten tombstones, several unlettered, but probably belonging to a Mission. One name is striking—that of Mr. J. Fieldbrave. It has been suggested that this may possibly have been the name given to an Indian Christian as a reward for an act of gallantry performed during the Mutiny. Records of the American Methodist Episcopal Mission show that a branch was established in Husainabad in the winter of 1858, the two missionaries living in the Asafi and Kala Kothis until 1866. This must have been their ultimate resting place, for one stone records the death of Eldore Noyes Messmore who died in 1869 aged five. The Rev. J. Messmore, who was a missionary in Lucknow for many years, erected the English Church in Lal Bagh.

After 1866 the Mission moved to Lal Bagh and Inayat Bagh ; for, when the ground surrounding the Machhi Bhawan was cleared, the local population naturally decreased.

The Victoria Park near here is one of the many "lungs" where Lucknow prides herself that her citizens may breathe air less congested than that of the narrow and tortuous streets of the city.

Green lawns shaded by fine trees now undulate in all innocence where once broken ground and narrow alleys and courts concealed dark crimes and their perpetrators. Here thief met thief to plan assault upon rich and unsuspecting citizens. Here they met again to compare notes and to argue through the night upon division of the loot. In 1890 the trustees of the wealthy Husainabad Endowment Fund took over the ground to convert it into a park. There now stands a bronze statue of Queen Victoria erected in her Jubilee year.

Beyond the park lies the Chowk entered by the Gol Darwaza which once bore great elephants upon either flank. Asaf-ud-Doulah built the Chowk at the end of the 18th century. This is a typical Indian bazaar street, furrowed and rutted, the houses unbelievably narrow and rising to a height out of all proportion to the width. Here jewellers and silver filigree workers ply their trade; pearl merchants unwrap from tiny scraps of rag dozens, nay hundreds, of fine pearls and the finest of soft silks set off with golden embroidery.

Through the ages an Indian bazaar never changes. It is, as it always has been, simply a collection of shops, generally in a narrow street, and for the most part containing similar articles. It is a lane full of small shops, with open fronts, where its men expose their wares and invite the passers-by to try them. The shops appear small from the confined frontage. Yet enter one of them and you discover room after room filled with merchandise. You go upstairs and downstairs to the right hand and to the left, and find nothing but goods, save a salesman who is ready to take his oath on "Ganga ka pani" that the worst article in his shop is the best of its kind.

SCARCE-REMEMBERED PLACES

MANY historical places in Lucknow are too small to be recognised as "protected monuments" though they are none the less interesting for that. They are in peril of sinking into oblivion, if they have not already crumbled literally to dust.

The Wingfield Park owes its conception to Sir George Campbell,

Judicial Commissioner of Oudh, who in 1860 caused some eighty acres to be converted into a park as a memorial to Sir Charles Wingfield who died during his tenure as Chief Commissioner.

Originally a walled garden occupied the site and was known as the Banarsi or Benares Bagh because of certain plants brought there from Benares. Where the marble *baradari* now stands, was a double-storeyed summer-house, and some of the statuary in the park once adorned the Kaiser Bagh Palaces.

Not far away on the left bank of the river stood the Chakkar Kothi or Round House, bombarded in 1858 from a battery erected on the site of the present Race Bungalow, by order of Sir James Outram. Soon after noon, on March 9, 1858, Sir Colin Campbell, who was standing on the roof of Dilkusha Palace, saw to his astonishment the regimental colour of the Bengal Fusiliers floating above the Chakkar Kothi which he believed to be in enemy occupation. It transpired that part of this regiment had taken the house after a short sharp fight.

About an hour later Lieutenant Butler, an officer of the Bengal Fusiliers, swam across the river which was there about sixty yards wide and running with a swift current. He penetrated into the canal works and found evidence of hasty desertion. He mounted the wall which stood exposed to hot fire from both sides. Eventually he attracted the attention of Sir Colin Campbell who was watching developments from the vantage point of the Martiniere and who sent a detachment of the 4th Punjabis to occupy the position. Lieutenant Butler was afterwards awarded the V.C.

The present cantonment was filled with parks and country houses belonging to the King and his courtiers. The house now used as an Officers' Mess by a British Infantry regiment was once the country residence of the Prime Minister of Oudh. It is characterised by a fine circular domed entrance hall ornamented with stucco designs similar to the mural decorations of La Martinière College.

The Muhammad Bagh was a large walled garden extending over both polo grounds, the present club grounds, and the Presbyterian Church. It adjoined Dilkusha Park near the junction of the present Tombs and Dilkusha Roads, at which corner Sir James Outram caused a battery to be entrenched on March 8, 1858.

On the present Brigade parade ground lay the village of Ghaili where, on December 21, 1875, Outram's spies informed him that a large force of 4,000 infantry, 400 cavalry and four guns, was drawn up with the intention of surrounding him. Accordingly, Outram divided his force which consisted of 1,200 infantry, 190 cavalry and six guns, into two. To the right lay a column under Colonel Purnell of the 90th Foot: to the left another under Colonel Guy of the 5th Fusiliers. Both advanced simultaneously to the attack, taking the enemy by surprise, routing them completely, and capturing all four guns with scarcely a casualty. The retreating force left some sixty dead on the field.

Jamaita was the name of another village situated on the Mall where the District and Brigade offices stand and extending over the site of the gymnasium.

The Char Bagh garden occupied a large area now covered by railway buildings. Clustered around the Kaiser Bagh the remains of many interesting buildings still linger among those of more recent erection. There stood the Kothi Dilruba Munzil, called after Dilruba Mahal, one of Wajid Ali Shah's wives. It belonged later to a Christian lady who died at Agra, and was occupied for many years by a Government pensioner named Piggott.

Near it the Bait-ul-Insha, or Correspondence Office, was so named by Wajid Ali Shah; but a couplet engraved over the door states that the house was built in 1240 A.H. or 1824 A.D., during the reign of Ghazi-ud-Din Haider. In the same area the Bait-ul-Iqra, or Office of Issue, was named by Wajid Ali Shah.

Within the Kaiser Bagh quadrangle stands the Qasr-ul-Buka, a striking pavilion of white marble. Built by one of the Kings of Oudh, it was originally an *imambara*, a place where meetings are held to mourn the deaths of Imam Hussain and his followers at Kerbala. The name Qasr-ul-Buka means "house of mourning." The building now belongs to the British Indian Association. The hall is hung with protraits of successive presidents of the Association and is used for social functions and public meetings.

THE SHAH NAJAF

IN THE SHAH NAJAF, OPPOSITE the Carlton Hotel, lie the remains of King Ghazi-ud-Din and his wives. It is alternatively known by the name of Najaf Ashraf, Najaf being the name of the town in Iraq where Moslem pilgrims of the Shia sect go to visit the tomb of Ali.

Ghazi-ud-Din Haider who reigned between 1814 and 1827

was the seventh and last Nawab of Oudh, for Lord Hastings raised him to the dignity of King in about 1818, thus promoting Lucknow to the status of a royal city.

Ghazi-ud-Din's favourite wife Mubarak Mahal (the Blessed Palace) was a European, whose real name was Miriam. According to custom Ghazi-ud-Din Haider built the Shah Najaf as his own mausoleum and his tomb of silver lies in the centre of the building, flanked by the larger and more imposing silver and gold tomb of Mubarak Mahal on one side and by a small tomb of another of his wives on the other. Still another wife is said to be buried in a corner of the main chamber.

Low white walls encircle the Shah Najaf and an imposing entrance opens on to a tended rose garden. In the centre, wide cloisters enclose a paved courtyard, and the entrance to the tomb is on the far side of the court.

At the top of a short flight of white marble steps stand finely carved sheesham wood doors from Burma. Immediately inside hang three contemporary protraits by Mrs. Jopling Rowe, of Ghazi-ud-Din and two of his successors. The walls are decorated with gilt mirrors and old pictures of Ali's horse, Duldul, drawn in the writing of the Koran. The King was a rich man and endowed his tomb with a crore of rupees lent in perpetuity to the British Government. Twice a year, at the Moharram festival and on the anniversary of the death of Mubarak Mahal, it is illuminated, special prayers are said and alms distributed to the poor.

In 1857 the Shah Najaf was a stronghold of the mutineers and stood in the direct route of the relieving force of Sir Colin Campbell. On the evening of November 15 the look-out man on the

Residency Tower received the signal "Advance to-morrow" semaphored from the top of the Martinière.

Accordingly on the 16th, Sir Colin with his force of some three thousand men advanced against about sixty thousand strongly entrenched rebels, and successfully drove them from the Sikandar Bagh. Following a brief halt they advanced on the Shah Najaf. After a three hours' bombardment even the naval guns of the *Shannon* could effect no breach in the solid walls. Sir Colin called his men to the charge and the Naval Brigade, the 93rd Highlanders and a detachment of the 90th Foot commanded by Captain (afterwards Field-Marshal Lord) Wolseley, made a gallant effort to scale the walls. Darkness was falling and success seemed impossible when Sergeant Paton of the 93rd Highlanders found an old breach. In poured the men. As they entered the mutineers bolted out of the far side. The British troops bivouacked there for the night.

Since then the ravages of war have been repaired, and no trace of the savage fighting remains. Indeed, between the mausoleum and the river Gumti lies a little building hung with curious old portraits of former kings and forgotten maulanas and wazirs, which seem to have been there since the day they were painted, so complete is the musty atmosphere of forgotten splendours of the Court of the Kings of Oudh.

THE SHER DARWAZA

On the road leading from Sa'adat Ali Khan's tomb to the gardens crowned with the white marble statue of Queen Victoria stands an unpretentious gateway once known as the Sher Darwaza or Tiger Gateway. About a hundred years ago it gave on to a courtyard. . A labyrinth of tiny streets and alleys wove around the rickety houses ; crazy steps led to pools of stagnant water. Dirt and disease lurked in every corner. Near the gateway stood a building dedicated to the twelve Imams, the descendants of Ali, the son-in-law of the Prophet.

When the British Raj assumed control of Oudh, this net-work of dwellings was swept away leaving only the Sher Darwaza, its name changed by violent circumstances into Neill's Gateway.

Brigadier-General J. G .S. Neill, C.B., A.D.C. to the Queen, belonged to the 1st Madras Fusiliers. The year 1857 found him with his "Lambs" sent from Calcutta to deal with the recalcitrant inhabitants of Benares, Allahabad and Cawnpore. He finally arrived in Lucknow with the first relief column.

At half past eight on the morning of September 25, 1857, the advance sounded, and Neill's Brigade, headed by Maude's Battery and two companies of the 5th Fusiliers, led the column and moved off from the Alam Bagh towards the Yellow House. At Char Bagh they were checked by the canal the bridge over which was strongly held by the rebels. In the confined streets there was only room for two of Maude's guns to come into action and the gunners suffered heavily under fierce fire. Maude and his subaltern, Maitland, both took active part in firing the guns.

Young Havelock, son of the General and A.D.C. to his father, was standing nearby when Maude called out that he could not hold out much longer. Young Havelock rode over to General Neill with the message, but the General refused to attack without authority, saying, "General Outram must turn up soon."

The story goes that the son wheeled his horse and galloped in the direction where his father was supposed to be. In a few suspiciously short minutes, he returned, bringing a verbal "message" that General Neill was to carry the bridge at once. Another version says that Colonel Fraser Tytler, D.A.Q.M.G. of the column, persuaded Neill to attack. In any case, the 1st Madras Fusiliers were ordered to assault.

Lieutenant W. D. Arnold dashed on to the bridge closely followed by his own men and a few of the 84th. Tytler and Lieutenant Havelock also galloped up but Tytler's horse was killed under him. Havelock escaped unscathed although he stood dismounted in the middle of the bridge waving his sword and encouraging his men. Arnold was shot in both thighs, but was made happy in the knowledge that the charge led by him carried the bridge and assured the success of the day.

On Septmber 27, Mr. Thornhill of the Bengal Civil Service, who had been in the Residency all through the siege, volunteered to go and bring in the wounded. He had previously been Assistant Commissioner of Lucknow and knew his way about. Somehow, having collected as many of the wounded as he could he lost his way back to the Residency and by mistake guided the long chain of *doolis*, filled with helpless wounded men, into the square near the Sher Darwaza. Here they were set upon, many being murdered. The insurgents set fire to the *doolies* so that many poor sufferers were burned to death.

Directly Mr. Thornhill had realised his mistake he rushed back to stop the rear of the column from entering the square, but as he ran he was wounded for the third time during the siege in the arm and eye. He died on October 12. Lieutenant Arnold, wounded on the Char Bagh Bridge, was lying in one of the *doolies* carried into Doolie Square, and although he escaped massacre, he died a few days later. Two private soldiers, Ryan and McManus, made heroic efforts to save him, both being awarded the V.C. Lieutenant Arnold is believed to have been the son of the famous Dr. Arnold, Headmaster of Rugby.

The next day the site was again the scene of fierce fighting. As the evening wore on, from the top of the Sher Darwaza a shot was fired which mortally wounded General Neill. At the place where he fell stands a small monument inscribed "*Dulce et decorum est pro patria mori*", with the name of Neill and the manner of his death.

At Ayr where his family trace their descent from the 16th century, a memorial describes him as "a brave, resolute, self-reliant soldier, universally acknowledged as the first who stemmed the torrent of rebellion in Bengal. Over his remains a memorial has been erected in the Residency cemetery to the officers and men of the 1st Madras Fusiliers who fell with him in Lucknow.

Further along Neill's Road, nearly opposite the Kothi Nur Bakhsh, stands a memorial inscribed with several names.

On June 3, 1857, the 41st Native Infantry mutinied at Sitapur and killed Colonel Birch their commanding officer and other officers, before making off to Fatehgarh. The other regiments in Sitapur immediately followed suit. The Europeans who remained made the best of their way across the river. Fourteen men, women and children reached Lucknow on June 8 and 10, but others who took refuge with Raja Lone Singh at Mitauli were turned out by him on August 6, and wandered about evading capture in the jungles until the end of October, when some three hundred of the Raja's troops arrested them.

Sir Mountstuart Jackson, aged nineteen, Assistant Commissioner of Sitapur, Captain Patrick Orr and Lieutenant Burnes were loaded with irons. They and the women and children with them, including one of Sir Mountstuart's two sisters, who had only lately arrived in India, were taken to Lucknow. There they were imprisoned in a tiny hovel within the Kaiser Bagh. On November 16 the men were taken away and shot by some of the deserters from the 71st Regiment.

Mrs. Harris, in her diary of the siege written within the Residency, says on June 27: "Eleven persons, ladies and gentlemen, escaped from Seetapore and are hiding in the jungles protected by a Rajah who is very civil to them, and the two Miss Jacksons and their brother are among them. It was positively asserted that they had been killed at Seetapore, the natives declaring they had seen their bodies, which leads one to hope that others may be found alive some day."

In 1858 Mrs. Harris added a postscript: "Only one of the Miss Jacksons escaped with her brother: the other was taken by a Rajah and has never been since heard of. Sir M. Jackson and his poor sister are still prisoners in Lucknow."

THE SIKANDAR BAGH

THE SIKANDAR BAGH IS one of the more modern of Lucknow's historic remains. It was built by Wajid Ali Shah, the last King of Oudh, for his favourite wife Sikandar Mahal Begum.

In the days of its original glories, the Sikandar Bagh was laid out with gaily coloured flower beds, grouped round a pillared *baradari*, the whole enclosed by a stout wall which still stands save where a road has been driven through.

The three-storeyed entrance gate is in moderately good repair and bears two excellent specimens of the royal fish badge. Under some of the more sheltered archways, traces of richly coloured and finely executed stucco still hint at past glories.

The troops who undertook the first relief of Lucknow under Havelock came within sound of the gun on September 22 and two days later halted to rest after several sharp encounters, while Outram and Havelock discussed the arrangement for further advance. Finally Havelock decided to cross the canal at Char Bagh and to approach the Residency by way of the Sikandar Bagh and the Chatter Munzil. He ultimately accomplished this on September 25, to find that his relieving force was strong enough only to reinforce the besieged ; not to rescue them.

The second relief under Sir Colin Campbell moved off from the Martinière at 8 o'clock on the morning of November 16. They followed the course of the Gumti until they turned up a narrow lane leading to the Sikandar Bagh. Suddenly a murderous fire came from the Sikandar Bagh walls ; for a short time Campbell's troops were scarcely able to move from the congested space in which they found themselves. Presently the only company of the 53rd with the column took cover and returned the enemy fire, while Blunt's horse battery somehow struggled up the steep banks of the lane and galloped into the open. The opposing fire showed no signs of slackening. One bullet which passed through a gunner and killed him, went on to strike Sir Colin in the thigh.

For an hour the troops bombarded the Sikandar Bagh, solid walls stoutly resisting bullets, until a small breach, about three feet square and nearly four feet from the ground, was discerned near one of the corner bastions. Sir Colin ordered the advance. No sooner had the bugle sounded than the 4th Punjab Infantry, the 93rd Highlanders, and the 53rd charged forward in a glorious race to be first through the breach. It is a moot and much discussed point who actually was first, but it seems generally accepted that Captain Burroughs of the 93rd has good claim to the title. He is said to have jumped clear through the hole, followed by a Sikh of the 4th Punjab Infantry. Highlander and Sikh pressed forward, Lieutenant Cooper, Colonel Ewart, and Lieutenant Gordon Alexander, all of the 93rd, being well to the fore, while the main body of the attackers made for the entrance gates where some of the defenders were holding an earth-work.

The garrison rushed to shut the massive doors, but Mukarrab Khan, a sepoy of the 4th Punjab Infantry, thrust his left arm into the aperture. It was badly wounded, so he thrust his other arm into the space instead, only to have that too almost severed at the wrist. The delay allowed his comrades to collect in sufficient numbers to force the doors. But for his unhesitating bravery the tale of the Sikandar Bagh might have been very different. In the meantime, those who had entered through the breach were engaged in hand to hand fighting, slowly driving the defenders before them. Burroughs was stunned by a sword cut on his head, from which he recovered later in the day, but the others joined Lumsden's party from the main entrance. Lumsden himself fell dead as he shouted, "Come on, men! For the honour of

Scotland !" And Colonel Ewart captured the colours defended by two rebel officers both of whom he killed.

Both sides fought with desperate courage. Although the rebels made a stand as they rallied round the central pavilion, the British soldiers crying, "Remember Cawnpore," drove them to the corner building. This the rebels succeeded in holding until a gun was brought to force the heavy door and they could offer resistance no more.

The British casualties had been heavy, but the other side lost some two thousand men, all of whom lie buried in a large grave nearby, still distinguishable by the grassy mound covering it. A tablet marks the spot "where the wall of the Sikandar Bagh was breached in the assault on 16th November, 1857," while just above it is another "erected by the officers of 2nd Battalion Princess Louise's Argyll and Sutherland Highlanders in 1869 to commemorate the part taken by the 93rd (Sutherland Highlanders) in storming this breach." They also erected a monument a few yards from the breach in memory of the 165 members of the Regiment who were killed during the engagements.

Not far from the wall is another grave in which lies the remains of Lieutenant Francis Dobbs and five privates, all of the 1st Madras Fusiliers, who were killed in action while storming the Shah Najaf immediately after the capture of the Sikandar Bagh.

There is a tablet in Christ Church erected by the brother officers of Captain John Tower Lumsden and Lieutenant John Cape, both of the 30th Regiment, Bengal Native Infantry. Captain Lumsden was born in 1823, son of an Aberdeen advocate, and was attached as an interpreter to the 93rd. Had he lived, Colonel Ewart of the 93rd said that he would have recommended him for the V.C. According to Lord Roberts, Lumsden followed Ewart through the breach in the wall, but on that day of stress and battle who can say clearly what happened ? What matters it now, except that many valiant lives were lost on both sides ?

THE TALUQDARS' HALL, CLOCK TOWER AND DAULAT KHANA

PAST THE Great Imambara, through the Rumi Darwaza, on the right hand side of the road, lies the Husainabad Park wherein are several buildings of interest. The Taluqdars' Hall, a rectangular red brick building, characterised by ornamental *terra cotta*-coloured iron pillars, was built by King Muhammad Ali Shah, who reigned from

1837 to 1842. He it was who slept peacefully in a small room in the Chutter Munzil Palace, while the Begum was trying to install her adopted grandson Moona Jan on the throne, following the poisoning of Nasir-ud-Din Haider that same evening. The building is alternatively known as the Baradari, which means "room with twelve doors", *i. e.*, a reception room. Interesting are the three high flood marks on the outer wall of the porch, the highest being that of 1923. From the porch a wide flight of steps leads to the interior of the building, where several rooms are now used as offices and record rooms—the largest as an assembly room for the Taluqdars of Oudh.

Round this room hang ten portraits, the work of two artists, depicting the rulers of Oudh, beginning with Nawab Sa'adat Khan and ending with King Wajid Ali Shah, who was deposed and sent to Calcutta where he died in 1887 at the age of sixty-seven. It is interesting to note the changes apparent from generation to generation. Sa'adat Khan was a strong purposeful man with a long cruel nose. Gradually the stature of the rulers dwindled, their countenances became less those of men of character and more of men who led dissolute lives. Each one is loaded with magnificent ropes of pearls and other priceless jewels.

The banqueting hall gives on to a spacious verandah looking out on the Husainabad Tank, a prosaic enough name for the lovely sheet of water. It too was built by Muhammad Ali Shah. It is well stocked with fish. Tradition has it that it was originally connected with the river. Now only occasional pairs of geese or jumping fish disturb its placid green depths. Reflected on its surface is the Husainabad Clock Tower, an ugly structure built in 1881 at a cost of nearly Rs. 20,000 donated by the Trustees of the Husainabad Endowment from the income on a legacy of thirty-six lakhs of rupees bequeathed by Muhammad Ali Shah for the upkeep of the lesser Imambara. A chime of five bells announces the hour quarters shown by the clock which is said to be the largest in India, and which has an ingenious lighting system.

On the opposite side of the lake, behind a belt of trees, stands an unfinished structure known as the Sat Khanda, or Seven-Storeyed Tower. This also was built by Muhammad Ali Shah, but he died when only four storeys had been completed, so the work on it was abandoned, and it stands to this day an unfinished memorial to this eighth ruler of Oudh, who spent large sums in making the Husainabad a broad and handsome street. Towards the end of his reign he was almost completely bed-ridden. It was his intention to be carried up the circular staircase of the Sat Khanda, now crumbling to dust, and there to lie upon the roof. There he could watch his plans for the beautifying of Husainabad mature.

Within the same little park stands a gateway leading to the Daulat Khana—a name embracing a collection of buildings—which means "Nobleman's Mansion." Several of these houses are of handsome aspect and are in good repair, although now surrounded by bazaar hovels. They were the original dwellings of Asaf-ud-Doulah and his court who took up their abode there when they transferred themselves and their capital from Fyzabad to Lucknow in 1775.

This group of buildings escaped the rough passage of the Mutiny, except for the Daulat Khana, which was occupied without resistance on March 17, 1858, by Sir James Outram's advancing force.

THE TARA WALA KOTHI

THE TARA WALA KOTHI, now the Imperial Bank building, was built by direction of Nasir-ud-Din Haider, King of Oudh, who reigned between 1827 and 1837, and under the supervision of Colonel Wilcox, his Astronomer Royal.

It was fitted with astronomical instruments. Colonel Wilcox

fulfilled his duties until his death in 1847, when King Muhammad Ali Shah who had succeeded his nephew allowed the post to fall into abeyance. Who Colonel Wilcox was is not known, save that he was a pensioner in Oudh. He was the last person known to have been buried in the old graveyard near Aminabad.

Nasir-ud-Din Haider did not lead a particularly exemplary life. His reign was marked by increasing signs of degeneracy. Several Europeans were in his employ, perhaps the most notorious being the famous barber, de Roussett, who exercised the most pernicious influence over the King. The King made not a murmur even when the barber's monthly bill measured four and a half yards in length and amounted to more than ninety thousand rupees, then the equivalent of nine thousand pounds.

It may well be imagined that but few records remain of the more sober activities of his time. Some years later the Tara Wala Kothi was used for the local courts of civil justice. Gubbins, who describes it as a handsome and classically designed building, says that it was protected by a regular guard of Native Infantry while several European officials occupied detached residences nearby.

In the insurrection of 1857 one Chimad Ullah Shah, an influential Moulvi of Fyzabad, adopted the Tara Wala Kothi as a meeting place for the rebel parliament. This Moulvi was usually known as Dunka (Drumbeat) Shah, for he employed a man to walk in front of him beating a drum wherever he went.

During the second relief of Lucknow, the Tara Wala Kothi was in the direct line of advance. From the sand-bagged roof the relieving force knew that the enemy were resolved to defend it. The guns of the *Shannon* forced a passage hard by the 32nd Mess

House but the sailor gunners were obliged to retire, owing to heavy musketry fire from the roof of the Tara Wala Kothi. On November 17, however, Sir Colin Campbell's relieving force made heroic onslaughts upon the 32nd Mess House. At three o'clock it was captured, as was the Tara Wala Kothi, and volumes of smoke issued from its lofty windows. With the capture of these two buildings the third line of the enemy's defence was broken and their courage shaken. About six thousand of them saw that their line of retreat was in danger of being cut off, so they fled towards the Cheenee Bazar and the Kaiser Bagh.

During the Mutiny the astronomical instruments all disappeared. Only hearsay tells that once a brass pillar stood in the central chamber and reared its head through the roof. To this day a pillar stands close to the house, sole survivor of the appliances in use when the building fulfilled its original purpose.

Although the Fyzabad Moulvi does not appear by name in the records of the hand to hand fighting round the Tara Wala Kothi, he is again heard of on February 15, 1858, when he led a strong body of horse and foot against the British forces. Major Olpherts galloped up with two guns and a troop of the military train and repulsed the attack, in which the Moulvi was severely wounded. Soon afterwards he returned undaunted to Lucknow with a large force and two guns, and occupied a strongly fortified position in the city. On March 21, a force consisting of parties of the 93rd Highlanders and the 4th Punjab Rifles was sent against him, and after a hundred and fifty of his men had been killed in a short but exceedingly sharp encounter, he and his remaining men fled. Although they were pursued for about six miles, the Moulvi himself escaped and disappeared into oblivion.

Years later the building, which consists of very few, very large and very lofty rooms, was restored and the existing bank premises were added. Early in October 1923, there were serious floods, and Mr. Davis, the occupant of the house, woke up one night to find that the water had risen half way up the entrance door. Immediately, with the help of two others, he constructed a raft of boxes, in case the water should rise higher before morning. For about a fortnight the building was isolated: staff and clients having to be ferried to and from the Mall by boat.

Wide lawns and shady trees now set off the stately and spacious building, characteristic of the years when the Kingdom of Oudh was of some account in the oriental world, and before the degeneration of luxury signed the death warrant upon the fortunes of the dissolute kings.